Chocolate Recipes

for Beginners

100+ DELICIOUS CREATIONS SUCH AS
BARS, TRUFFLES AND BROWNIES

TABLE OF CONTENTS

20 Health Benefits of Chocolate

Chocolate is regarded as an indulgent treat because it is mainly associated with weight gain and acne. Americans spend $10 billion annually on chocolaty treats. It is not all bad news as countless studies show dark chocolate has many health benefits. Here are 20 you may not know about and which will help you to indulge in it with less guilt. In moderation of course – I mean, the guilt!

1. It can help your heart to stay healthy

Lots of studies reveal that the flavonoids in chocolate can help your veins and arteries to stay supple. Over 7 studies followed 114,000 participants who were given a few servings of dark chocolate a week. The results showed that their risk of getting a heart attack was reduced by about 37% while the chances of getting a stroke were 29% less when they had a higher consumption of chocolate.

2. It may help improve your memory as you get older

Research has shown that when elderly people were given specially prepared cocoa extracts which was high in flavanols, their cognitive function greatly improved. The only problem is that when it comes to eating chocolate, the percentage of those cocoa flavanols is much reduced due to the processing and the addition of eggs, sugar and milk.

3. It can help to avoid sunburn

One study conducted in London found that women who were given chocolate with a high flavanol content were able to withstand double the amount of UN light on their skins without burning, compared to those on lower doses.

4. It may make you better at math

I was never good at math at school. Maybe I should have eaten more dark chocolate! This is the startling conclusion I have reached after reading about the research of Professor David Kennedy who is Director of Brain, Performance and Nutrition at the Research Center of Northumbria University (UK). Participants were given 500 mg of flavanols in a hot cocoa drink. They benefited from increased flow to the brain as a result and were better at coping with difficult math equations.

5. It may put you in a better mood

I wish my uncle had given my aunt some chocolate when he told her to stop crying and to 'cheer up.' He obviously had not read about the work at the University of Swinburne in Australia. These guys again targeted the cocoa polyphenols and they found that it had a beneficial effect on the mood of the participants who were calmer and happier.

6. It may help lower cholesterol levels

The Journal of Nutrition carries an interesting article about the results of a study done to determine whether dark chocolate could have any effect on the LDL cholesterol levels. They found that when subjects were given bars of dark chocolate with plant sterols and flavanols, they were getting lower scores on their cholesterol levels.

7. It may help people with Alzheimer's disease

As we know, the nerve pathways to the brain get damaged when Alzheimer's disease strikes, causing severe loss in certain mental functions. It is fascinating to read about how one extract from cocoa, called lavado, can actually reduce the damage done to these vital pathways.

8. It can help you with your workout

Another magical flavanol in chocolate is epicatechin. Mice were given this substance and they were much fitter and stronger than those mice on water only. Researchers say that to get the best results from your workout you have to limit the amount to only about half of one square of chocolate a day! If you have too much, it could undo the beneficial effects.

9. It is very nutritious

Did you know that if choose chocolate with a high cocoa content (75% to 85%) you are getting a very nutritious snack? Take the typical 100 gram chocolate bar. It has almost all of your RDA for copper and manganese. It contains over half your magnesium RDA and about two thirds (67%) of your RDA for iron. It also has about 10% of fiber. There is also lots of zinc, selenium and potassium too.

10. It can help to lower your blood pressure

You may not know it but having the right amount of NO (Nitric Oxide) in your body can help your arteries to relax. That will, in turn help to take some of the pressure off them and the result is a lower BP count. Just another benefit of the dark chocolate flavanols which help to produce this vital Nitric Oxide.

11. It helps you produce more endorphins

When you are on a high, it may be due to excitement, love or after exercise. This high is due to the release of endorphins which are brain hormones. The great advantage of chocolate is that flavanols can also help in endorphin production without having to run a marathon! Endorphins play a key role in helping to prevent depression and other mental disorders.

12. It may reduce pregnancy complications

One of the complications of pregnancy is known as preeclampsia in which blood pressure can shoot up. Researchers have established that one of the chemicals in dark chocolate, theobromine, can stimulate the heart and help the arteries dilate. When pregnant women were given higher doses of chocolate, they had a 40% less chance of developing this complication.

13. It may help with diabetes

You probably think that chocolate is too sweet for diabetics and is one of their banned treats, but one small study at the University of L'Aquila in Italy found that the right does of chocolate flavonoids can help the body's metabolism and enhance insulin function. This could benefit people with diabetes but more studies need to be done.

14. It may help you reduce your food cravings

You know the feeling: you cannot function until you have a snack. One of the healthiest is a piece of dark chocolate because it fills you up quicker and reduces craving for salty and sweet snacks, according to a small research study.

15. It may help your cough

Another marvelous effect of the theobromine chemical in chocolate is that it can calm a troublesome cough. Manufacturers are looking at this to produce safer cough syrups instead of using codeine which has some undesirable side effects.

16. It may help with blood circulation

Normally you take an aspirin to help prevent blood clotting and to improve circulation. Studies now show that chocolate can have a similar effect.

17. It can also help you see better

University of Reading researchers were curious to see if dark chocolate flavanols could actually improve vision as they knew it certainly improved blood circulation in general. They decided to do a small experiment and gave two groups of volunteers some white and dark chocolate. The dark chocolate groups were doing better on vision tests afterwards.

18. It may help reduce fatigue

If you suffer from chronic fatigue syndrome you should try adding chocolate to your daily diet. One group of sufferers were given a daily dose of chocolate for two months. They were less tired and the best news of all is that they did not put on any extra weight.

19. It may help to lower your Body Mass Index

There has been a lot of emphasis on how chocolate can actually reduce your BMI (Body Mass Index) which is how you measure up as regards your height versus your weight. One study took 1,000 Californians and they found that those who ate chocolate more often during the week had a lower BMI. Overall diet and exercise regimes were not factors which influenced this result.

20. It may help reduce your chances of getting cancer

As we have mentioned, the cocoa flavanols in dark chocolate have both anti-inflammatory and antioxidant properties. These are important in keeping the actions of free radicals at bay. As we know, these are the protagonists when cancer starts to invade cells.

Now that you have finished the list, why not have a piece of dark chocolate and enjoy it? Remember, the darker the better!

Let's Start!

Truffles

Marshmallow Puffs

36 large marshmallows 1-1/2 C semisweet chocolate chips 1/2 C chunky peanut butter 2 T butter or margarine

Makes 3 dozen

Line a 9-in. square pan with foil and butter the foil. Arrange marshmallows in pan. In a double boiler or microwave-safe bowl, melt chocolate chips, peanut butter and butter. Pour over the marshmallows. Chill completely. Cut between marshmallows

Honey Balls for Passover

1/2 C honey 1/3 C sugar 1 1/4 C chopped walnuts 1/4 C matzo farfel 2 tsp. grated orange or lemon zest

Makes 18-24

In a medium sized saucepan over low heat, heat the honey and sugar to boiling. Stir constantly. Add the nuts and the farfel and stir until the mixture is thick. Add the grated zest. Remove from heat and drop by teaspoonful onto a wet cookie sheet or wax paper, forming small balls. Cool.

Nariation: Roll the balls in finely grated nuts or coconut.

Quick & Easy Microwave Peanut Butter Fudge

12 oz. semisweet chocolate chips 12 oz. peanut butter 14 oz. sweetened condensed milk

Makes approximately 42 pieces

In a 1-1/2 quart microwave-proof bowl, melt chocolate and peanut butter on high power for 3 minutes. Stir well. Add milk and stir until well blended. Pour mixture into 8x8 dish lined with waxed paper. Refrigerate to chill.

Rum Balls

1 3/4 cups vanilla wafer cookie crumbs 1 cup ground pecans 1 cup confectioners sugar 1/4 cup cocoa 3 tablespoons light
corn syrup 1/4 cup light rum 1/3 cup confectioners' sugar (for dipping)

Makes About 2 1/2 Dozen

Mix all ingredients, except for 1/3 cup confectioners sugar. Roll into one inch balls. Roll balls in remaining confectioners sugar to coat.

White Chocolate Apricot-Hazelnut Truffles

(makes 28 truffles)

Ingredients:
1 1/4 C hazelnuts (aka filberts)
1/4 C finely chopped dried apricots 24 ounces imported white chocolate 6 Tbl heavy cream

Instructions:
On a baking sheet, spread out 1 1/4 C hazelnuts. Bake at 350 F for 10 minutes, or until nuts are light brown and the dark skins are cracked. Remove as much of the skins as possible by rubbing nuts in a terry- cloth towel. Finely chop nuts in a food processor.

In a 1-quart glass container, combine 12 ounces imported white chocolate, cut up and 6 Tbl heavy cream.

[Note: I used the Nestle white chocolate chips that are available in my local supermarket. It worked well, but I am sure it would be better if you use a good import instead.]

Microwave mixture on MEDIUM (70% power), 3 to 4 minutes, stirring twice, until chocolate is melted and smooth. [You can do this step in a double-boiler if you don't have a microwave.]

Stir into melted chocolate 3/4 C of the chopped nuts and 1/4 C finely chopped dried apricots.

Cover the mixture and refrigerate 1 to 2 hours, or until mixture is firm enough to hold its shape. (If mixture gets too hard, let stand at room temperature for 30 minutes or so, until firm but soft enough to shape.) Form 28 smooth 1 1/4-inch diameter balls, either by using a 1 1/4- inch automatic-release ice cream scoop, or by rolling 1 Tbl of the mixture between your (clean!) hands.

Place on a wax paper-lined cookie sheet and refrigerate until firm, 1 hour or longer.

Easy Truffles

(Servings: 64) Ingredients:

8 oz 1/3 c 1/3 c 2 ea 1/4 t 1 x

Semi-sweet chocolate Milk
Unsalted butter
Egg yolks, slightly beaten

Nanilla extract Unsweetened cocoa

Instructions:
In saucepan, melt chocolate with milk and butter over low heat, stirring until smooth. Remove from heat. Stir 1/4 cup hot mixture into egg yolks, the whisk yolks into chocolate mixture in saucepan. Add vanilla; beat well. Pour into small bowl; cover and refrigerate until firm. (You can store in refrigerator for up to 2 days at this point.)

Form teaspoonfuls into balls; roll in cocoa and shake off excess. Makes 1 pound (about 2 dozen). About 75 calories each.

For gift-giving: use a glass jar with lid or candy dish covered with plastic wrap. Store covered in refrigerator for 3 weeks and in freezer for up to 2 months.

Cognac Truffles

Ingredients:
3 1 oz square of unsweetened chocolate
1 1/4 c confectioners' sugar
1/3 c butter
3 egg yolks (I use the whites to make macaroons or meringue cookies)
1 tsp vanilla or 2 TBSP of cognac

Instructions:
Melt chocolate. Combine sugar and butter in bowl. Cream together. Add egg yolks, 1 at a time. Stir in melted chocolate and flavoring. Chill mixture. Break off pieces and form into balls. Roll in coating. Air-dry 1 hour. Store in air-tight container in very cool place. Makes about fifty truffles.

Suggested coatings: ground almonds or other nuts, cocoa, more melted chocolate, confectioners' sugar, coconut, chocolate or colored jimmies.

Note that this uses raw egg yolks. I find a melon baller to be very handy in forming the truffles.

Chocolate Anise Truffles

Ingredients:

1/4 cup 1/2 cup 12 oz. 2 cups

Anise liquor

butter
semi-sweet chocolate

pulverized anisette cookies

Instructions:
In a double boiler melt the chocolate, constantly stirring with a wooden spoon. When the chocolate has melted, add the butter and slowly stir it into the chocolate as it melts. Continue to stir for another minute until it is well mixed and smooth. Add in the Rum and stir until well mixed, then sprinkle in the pulverized anisette cookies (a little at a time, as sometimes it takes less) until the mixture is slightly thickened but still smooth. You want the mixture to remain as a thick sauce at this point.

When you have thoroughly mixed in the anisettes, rest the top of your double boiler in a bucket of ice and WHISK the truffle mixture slowly until it has cooled (about 15 minutes). Do not stop whicking or the butter and rum will separate out of the chocolate-anisette. When the sauce is completely cooled it should have a soft but solid consistency which you can then spoon out and form into truffles and coat with chocolate powder or confectioners sugar.

Bars

Babe Ruth Bars

1 cup peanut butter
1 cup white corn syrup
1/2 cup packed brown sugar 1/2 cup white sugar
6 cups cornflakes cereal
1 cup semisweet chocolate chips 2/3 cup peanuts

1 In a large saucepan over medium heat, combine the peanut butter, corn syrup, brown sugar and white sugar. Cook stirring occasionally until smooth. Remove from heat and quickly mix in the cornflakes, chocolate chips and peanuts until evenly coated.

2 Press the entire mixture gently into a buttered 9x13 inch baking dish. Allow to cool completely before cutting into bars.

Caramel Apples w/ Chocolate

Makes 8 apples
1 piece of Styrofoam
1 apples
8 ice cream sticks
12 packages (14 oz each) creamy caramels
2 tbs. water
3/4 cup pistachios, chopped
8 foil cupcake liners
3 ounces semisweet chocolate
Place Styrofoam on a flat surface. Lightly coat baking sheet with cooking spray. Remove stems from apples. Insert wooden stick into stem of each apple. Place caramels in saucepan. Add the water, heat stirring until caramels are melted. Working quickly with one apple at a time, and keeping caramel over low heat, dip the apple into the caramel, turning to coat the apple, remove the apple from the caramel and gently shake. Pat pistachios onto top of apple, place on prepared sheet. Refrigerate until caramel is cool. Heat chocolate in top of double boiler, until melted. Drizzle chocolate over apples. Press apples
sticks into Styrofoam. Refrigerate until the chocolate hardens. Remove from Styrofoam to foil cupcake liners

Chocolate Cake In A Jar

1 stick plus 3 T. butter or margarine 3 c. white sugar
4 eggs
1 T. vanilla

2 c. applesauce, unsweetened
3 c. white flour
3/4 c. unsweetened cocoa powder 1 tsp. baking soda

1/2 tsp. baking powder 1/8 tsp. salt

Prewash 8 pint-sized wide mouth canning jars (be sure to use the kind that have no shoulders) in hot, soapy water. Rinse well, dry and let them come to room temperature. Grease insides of jar well with butter.

Beat together butter, and half of sugar until fluffy. Add eggs and remaining sugar, vanilla and applesauce.

Sift dry ingredients together, and add to the applesauce mixture a little at a time. Beat well after each addition.

Pour 1 c. of batter into each jar, and carefully remove any batter from the rims.

Place jars in a preheated 325 oven, and bake for 40 mins.

While cakes are baking, bring a saucepan of water to a boil, and carefully add jar lids. Remove pan from heat, and keep lids hot until ready to use.

When the cakes have finished baking, remove jars from oven. Make sure jar rims are clean. (If they're not, jars will not seal correctly)

Place lids on jars, and screw rings on tightly. Jars will seal as they cool.

Cakes will slide right out when ready to serve. Eat within 1 month.

White Chocolate Pretzels

1 pkg. long pretzel rods
1 pkg. almond bark, or vanilla candy coating
Decorations, such as red and green sprinkles, holiday M&Ms or crushed up candy canes

Place the candy coating in a microwave-safe bowl. Make sure you do not get any water in the bowl. Any water at all will cause the candy coating not to melt properly and separate.

Microwave the candy coating for 1 min., then stir and microwave an additional min., until it is completely melted and smooth.

Stick a pretzel rod into the chocolate, and with a spoon, cover about 3/4 of the pretzel with chocolate. Let the excess drip back into the bowl.

Sprinkle the chocolate with either red and green colored sprinkles, crushed up peppermints, or stick red and green M&Ms to the chocolate.

Place the decorated pretzel on a piece of waxed paper or aluminum foil, and let it dry completely, about 1 hr. Gently pull the pretzels off the paper.

25.) Pretzel Bouquet

Lay about 10 White Chocolate Pretzels on a sheet of red or green tissue paper.

Wrap the pretzels up like a bouquet of roses would be wrapped, and tie red, green and white curling ribbon around the middle to secure.

With scissors, curl the ribbon, then tie on a small gift card.

26.) Pretzels In A Glass

Find a tall glass, such as a parfait glass, or one of those neat glasses mixed drinks are served in.

Pour some holiday candies, such as M&Ms or hard mints, in the bottom of the glass. Put as many pretzels as you can in the glass sitting on the candies, but leave a little room for them to move around, so they don't break when they are pulled out.

Cover the top of the glass with a piece of colored plastic wrap, or you can cut a piece of holiday fabric, and double the width of the top with pinking shears to cover.

Tie a pretty ribbon around the glass to secure, and you have a neat gift for someone special!

Mocha Fondue

Update chocolate fondue with a hint of coffee, and serve it with meringue cookies as crispy dippers.

1 4-ounce package sweet baking chocolate, broken up 4 ounces semisweet chocolate, chopped
2/3 cup light cream or milk
1/2 cup sifted powdered sugar

1 teaspoon instant coffee crystals
2 tablespoons coffee liqueur
Assorted fruits (such as star fruit slices, pineapple chunks, kiwi fruit wedges, strawberries, pear slices, banana slices) Meringue cookies

1. In a heavy saucepan combine chocolates, cream, sugar, and coffee crystals. Heat and stir over low heat until melted and smooth. Remove from heat; stir in liqueur. Pour into a fondue pot; keep warm over low heat. Serve with fruit and cookies. Makes 6 to 8 servings.

Oatmeal, Peanut Butter, and Chocolate Chunk Cookies

3/4 cup butter, softened
3/4 cup peanut butter
1-1/4 cups packed brown sugar
1-1/4 cups granulated sugar
1-1/2 teaspoons baking powder
1/2 teaspoon baking soda
3 eggs
1-1/2 teaspoons vanilla
2-1/4 cups all-purpose flour
2-2/3 cups rolled oats
1 10-ounce package miniature milk chocolate kisses

1. Beat butter and peanut butter in a large mixing bowl with an electric mixer on medium to high speed for 30 seconds. Add granulated sugar, brown sugar, baking powder, and baking soda; beat until combined, scraping sides

of bowl occasionally. Beat in eggs and vanilla until combined. Beat in flour. Stir in rolled oats with a wooden spoon. Stir in chocolate kisses. 2. Drop dough from a #50 or #60 scoop, or from a tablespoon, 3 inches apart

onto an ungreased cookie sheet. Slightly flatten dough with your hand, if desired. Bake in a 375 degree F oven about 8 to 10 minutes or until edges are lightly browned. Transfer to wire racks and cool. Store in an airtight container or plastic bag at room temperature up to 3 days. Makes 60 to 72 cookies.

Make-Ahead Tip: Cool cookies completely. In an airtight or freezer container, arrange cookies in a single layer; cover with a sheet of waxed paper. Repeat layers, leaving enough air space to close container easily. Freeze up to 1 month.

Rich chocolate brownies

Ingredients
3/4 cups flour
1/4 t. salt
1 1/2 squares unsweetened chocolate
1/2 c. margarine or butter
2 eggs
1 cup sugar
1 t. vanilla
1 ripe banana, well mashed
1/2 cup semi-sweet chocolate chips
1/2 cup broken walnut meats
No baking powder or soda. This makes them extra dense and moist. Directions
Preheat oven to 350 F, (325 for a glass pan). Combine flour and salt in a small
bowl. Set aside. Melt margarine or butter and unsweetened chocolate in a small
pan on low heat. Cool to room temperature. In a large bowl, beat eggs, sugar
and vanilla. Add mashed banana. Stir in chocolate mixture. Gradually sift and
stir in flour mixture. Add chocolate chips and walnuts. Pour
into an 8"x 8" pan that has been sprayed with Pam or cooking
oil. Bake for 30 to 35 minutes.

Mini Chocolate Chip Cheesecake Ball

INGREDIENTS:
1 8-ounce package cream cheese, softened 1/2 cup butter, softened
3/4 cup confectioners sugar
2 tablespoons brown sugar
1/2 teaspoon vanilla extract
3/4 cup mini semisweet chocolate chips 3/4 cup finely chopped pecans

DIRECTIONS:
In a medium bowl, beat together cream cheese and butter until smooth.
Mix in confectioners sugar, brown sugar and vanilla. Stir in chocolate chips.
Cover, and chill in the refrigerator for 2 hours. Shape chilled cream cheese
mixture into a ball. Wrap with plastic, and chill in the refrigerator for 1 hour or
overnight. Roll the cheese ball in finely chopped pecans before serving. Serve
with chocolate graham crackers.

Peanut Butter Bon Bons

1 1/2 c. graham cracker crumbs 1 c. peanut butter
1 c. melted oleo or butter
1 lb. powdered sugar

12 oz. milk chocolate chips 1/2 bar paraffin

Form crumbs, peanut butter, oleo and sugar into balls and freeze. Melt chips and paraffin in double boiler. Dip balls into chocolate mixture.

M&M'S® Holiday Brownies
A rich, colorful, layered treat that the family can help decorate.

What you'll need:
1 box your favorite brownie mix (for 13"x 9" baking pan) 1 bag M&M'S® Milk Chocolate Candies for the Holidays
2 8-ounce packages cream cheese
2/3 cup sugar
1/4 cup heavy cream
2 eggs
1/2 teaspoon vanilla extract
1 1/2 cups whipped cream (optional)

What to do:
Preheat the oven to 350 degrees.

Prepare the brownie mix according to the package directions. Spoon batter into 13" x 9" baking pan, spreading evenly.

Cover batter with 1 cup of M&M'S® Brand Milk Chocolate Candies for the Holidays.
In another mixing bowl, thoroughly beat the cream cheese with the sugar. Slowly add the heavy cream, eggs and vanilla extract. Blend mixture until smooth, scraping down the sides of the bowl several times.

Evenly spoon the cream cheese mixture over the brownie batter.

Bake for 50 to 60 minutes, or until a toothpick inserted into the center of the pan comes out almost clean.

Remove and cool completely.

Optional: Just before serving, top with a layer of whipped cream.
Cut into 2-inch squares.
Prior to serving, decorate with M&M'S® Brand Milk Chocolate Candies for the Holidays.
Refrigerate any leftovers.

Cream Cheese Brownies

INGREDIENTS:
4 ounce package German sweet chocolate 5 tablespoons butter
3 ounce package cream cheese
1 cup sugar
3 eggs
1/2 cup plus 1 tablespoon flour
1-1/2 teaspoons vanilla
1/2 teaspoon baking powder
1/4 teaspoon salt
1/2 cup nuts, chopped
1/4 teaspoon almond extract

TO PREPARE:
Melt chocolate with 3 tablespoons butter over low heat, stirring constantly. Cool. Cream remaining butter with cream cheese until
soft. Gradually add 1/4 cup sugar. Blend in 1 egg, 1 tablespoon
flour, and 1/2 teaspoon vanilla. Set aside.
Beat remaining eggs until thick. Gradually add remaining sugar. Add baking powder, salt, and remaining flour. Blend in cooled chocolate mixture, nuts, almond extract, and remaining vanilla. Measure 1 cup chocolate batter and set aside.
Spread remaining chocolate batter in a greased 9-inch square pan. Top with cheese mixture. Drop measured chocolate batter from tablespoon onto cheese mixture; swirl to marbleize. Bake at 350oF for 35 to 40 minutes. Cool. Cut and store in refrigerator.

YIELD: 18 squares

Cream Cheese Topped Brownies

Brownie Batter:

1 c. butter or margarine 2 c. sugar
2 tsp. vanilla extract
4 eggs

3/4 c. powdered baking cocoa (Hershey's or store brand) 1/2 tsp. baking powder
1/4 tsp. salt
1 c. flour

Cream Cheese Marbling:

1 egg
1/4 c. sugar
4 oz. pkg. cream cheese, softened

In a lg. mixing bowl combine in the following order: butter, 2 c. sugar, vanilla extract, 4 eggs, cocoa, baking powder, salt and flour.

Grease 9x13" baking pan. Pour batter into prepared pan.

Prepare the cream cheese topping: in a separate mixing bowl beat until smooth: 1 egg, 1/4 sugar and softened cream cheese.

Drop spoonfuls of the cream cheese mixture on the brownie batter. Run knife lengthwise across pan dragging through the cream cheese. Turn pan and drag knife again across the pan to marble the mixture, but not combine.

Bake in 350 oven for 30-35 mins. or until brownies just begin to pull away from sides of pan. Cool. Cut into bars.

Makes about 24 brownies

Eclair Cake

1 1 lb. box honey graham crackers**
2 small regular OR instant vanilla pudding* 2 3/4 c. milk
1 8 oz. container Cool Whip

Frosting:

1 can Duncan Hines Chocolate Buttercream frosting, softened for about 10 seconds in the microwave, so that it will spread easily across the top layer of the cake.
OR
1 pkg. Choco-bake (unsweetened liquid chocolate)
2 tsp. white Karo
2 tsp. vanilla
3 T. soft margarine
1 1/2 c. powdered sugar
3 T. milk

Butter 9x13" pan, and layer with whole graham crackers.

Prepare pudding according to pkg. direction, and let cool, or for instant pudding, mix pudding and milk. Blend in cool whip.

Put 1/2 pudding mixture over crackers. Layer more crackers over pudding. Top with rest of pudding. Cover with a layer of crackers. You will have 3 layers of crackers.

Refrigerate for 2 hrs. before frosting. Frosting:

Beat all frosting ingredients until smooth. Frost cake and refrigerate 2 hrs.

Cake can be frozen. Makes 10-16 servings

Note:
*Chocolate pudding can be used.
*French Nanilla pudding can be used. **Chocolate graham crackers can be used.

German Chocolate Chip Bread

2 boxes of German Chocolate cake mix
2 small boxes of chocolate instant pudding 1- 12 oz sour cream
10 eggs
1 1/2 cups of oil
1/2 cup of water
12 oz of chocolate chips
1 cup of chopped nuts (if desired)

Instructions:
Mix together all ingredients. Pour into three greased loaf pans. Bake at 325 degrees for one hour or until done when tested with wooden pick.

May be frozen, heated in microwave, and keeps well in refrigerator for several days.

Cadbury's Creme Egg

Serving Size: 12 Preparation Time: Categories:

1/2 cup light corn syrup 1/4 cup butter, softened 1 teaspoon vanilla
1/4 teaspoon salt

3 cups powdered sugar
4 drops yellow food coloring
2 drops red food coloring
1 bag milk chocolate chips (12 ounces) 2 tablespoons vegetable shortening

1) Combine the corn syrup, butter, vanilla, and salt in a large bowl. Beat well
with an electric mixer until smooth.
2) Add powdered sugar, one cup at a time, mixing by hand after each addition.
Mix well until creamy.

3) Remove about 1/3 of the mixture, and place it in a small bowl. Add the food
colorings, and stir well.
4) Cover both mixtures, and refrigerate for at least 2 hours, or
until firm.

5) When mixtures are firm, roll a small, marble-sized ball from the orange filling,
and wrap a portion of the white filling (approx. twice the size) around it. Form
this filling into the shape of an egg, and place it on a cookie sheet that has been
brushed with a light coating of vegetable shortening. Repeat process with the
remaining filling ingredients, then refrigerate these "eggs" for 3-4 hours, or until
firm.

6) Combine the milk chocolate chips with the shortening in a glass or ceramic
bowl. Microwave chocolate on HIGH for 1 minute, then stir, and microwave again
for 1 minute more; stir.
7) Use a fork to dip each center into the chocolate; tap the fork lightly on the side
of the bowl, then place each candy onto waxed paper. Chill.

8) after 1-2 hours of chilling, dip each candy once more, and chill for several
hours, or until completely firm.

Nienna Chocolate Bars

2 sticks butter
2 egg yolks
1 1/2 C sugar
2 1/2 C flour
1 (10 oz.) raspberry jelly (seedless) 1 C semi sweet chocolate chips

1/4 tsp. salt 4 egg whites

Preheat oven to 350. Cream butter with egg yolks and 1/2 cup sugar. Add flour and knead with fingers. Pat batter out with fingers on greased cookie sheet to about 3/8" thickness. Bake for

15 to 20 minutes until lightly browned. Remove from oven. Spread with jelly and top with chocolate chips. Beat egg whites and salt until
stiff peaks form. Fold in remaining cup of
sugar. Gently spread on top. Bake for
additional 24 minutes. Cool and cut into 2"x2" bars.

Black and White Chocolate Bars

1 lb Real white chocolate, melted 1 lb Chocolate chips; melted
3/4 c Evaporated milk
1/4 c margarine

1 ts Nanilla (or other extract)
1/2 c Toasted hazelnuts (or walnuts)

To ensure that the recipe will set up properly, do not use white baking confections that are not real white chocolate. The word "cocoa" should appear in the ingredients.

Line the inside of an 8" square baking pan with plastic wrap and set aside.

Toast nuts by placing on a cookie sheet and baking in pre-heated 350 degrees F. oven until skin begins to flake off. Remove skins by rubbing with a clean towel. Chop nuts with a knife, or pulse in a food processor.

Melt chocolate in a separate medium-sized bowls over double boilers. Combine and melt the evaporated milk and GoldùnùSoft margarine over medium heat. Remove from heat and reserve.

Add half the milk and margarine mixture to the melted chocolate chips. Mix well, pour into lined baking dish, an spread evenly. Refrigerate a few minutes.

Add balance of milk mixture to the melted white chocolate, then add the vanilla and mix until well blended.

Smoothly spread the mixture over the first layer and top with nuts. Refrigerate until firmly set (24 hrs.) and cut into bars. Store chilled.

Caramel Filled Chocolate Bars

1 German Chocolate cake mix 3/4 c Margarine, melted
14 oz Bag caramels
2/3 c Evaporated milk, divided 1 c Chocolate chips

1 c Walnuts, chopped
Melt caramels and 1/3 cup evaporated milk over hot water or in microwave, stirring every thirty seconds. Keep warm.
Mix the cake mix, margarine and 1/3 cup evaporated milk and beat well. Spread 1/2 the batter in a greased 9x13 inch pan. Bake for 6 minutes at 350 degrees. Cool about 2 minutes. Spread caramel mixture over baked layer and sprinkle with chocolate chips. Stir 1/2 cup nuts into remaining 1/2 of batter and drop by half teaspoonful over top. Sprinkle with remaining 1/2 cup nuts. Return to oven and bake for 18 minutes at 350 degrees. Cool in pan and cut into 1 1/2 inch squares.

Chewy Chocolate Orange Bars

2 c Cake flour
3/4 ts Baking powder
1/2 ts Salt
1 1/2 c Quick-cooking oats
1 c Dark-brown sugar, packed
2 Egg whites
Raisin Puree
3/4 c Chopped bittersweet chocolate
1/3 c Toasted walnuts, optional
1 tb Grated orange zest

Sift together flour, baking powder and salt into large bowl. Stir in oats and brown sugar. Beat egg whites lightly in another bowl. Stir in Raisin Puree. Stir into flour mixture along with chocolate, walnuts, and orange zest just until blended. Spoon in 9-inch-square baking pan sprayed with non-stick vegetable spray. Bake at 350 degrees F. 25 to 30 minutes. Cool. Cut into 24 bars.

Chocolate Bars

2 c All-purpose flour;
1 c Sugar;
1/2 c Cocoa;
1 ts Baking soda;
Dry substitute equal to 1/3 cup sugar 1/2 ts Cinnamon;

1/2 ts Salt;
1 c Margarine (2 Sticks); at room temperature
2 lg Eggs;
2 ts Nanilla;
1/2 c Semisweet chocolate chips;
Place flour, sugar, cocoa, baking soda, dry sugar substitute, cinnamon, and salt in a mixer bowl and mix a low speed to blend well. Add margarine, eggs, vanilla and water, and mix at medium speed to blend well. Spread batter evenly in an 11" by 15" jelly roll pan that has been sprayed with pan spray or greased with margarine. Bake at 325 degrees for 20 to 25 minutes, or until bars pull away the sides of the pan and a cake tester comes out clean from the center. Place on wire rack and sprinkle chocolate chips evenly over the top of the hot bars. Mark four by eight and cool until chocolate has hardened. Cut as marked. (Might be a good idea to cut even more sugar out of this.)

Chocolate Candy Bar

1 Envelope SF Hot Cocoa Mix 2 tb Cold water
2 tb Golden raisins; or -
1 ts Peanut butter; or

1 ts Chopped nuts
In small bowl stir cocoa mix with water. Save envelope that mix came in. Stir in raisins or peanut butter or nuts. Spoon mixture back into cocoa envelope. Fold over top and let stand against wall in bottom of freezer for about 4 hours. When frozen peel off envelope and eat. Tastes like fudge.

Chocolate Caramel Nut Bars

14 oz Bag caramels, remove wrappers
5 oz Can evaporated milk
1 Box German chocolate cake mix with pudding
1/2 c Margarine, melted
1 1/2 c Walnuts, chopped
6 oz Semisweet chocolate chips
Melt caramels with 1/3 cup milk in the microwave. Stir until smooth. Combine remaining milk, mix and margarine. Mix well. Press half of cake mixture into the bottom of a greased 13 x 9 baking pan. Bake 350 degrees for 6 minutes. Sprinkle with 1 cup walnuts, chocolate pieces over the crust; top with caramel mixture spreading to the edges of the pan. Top with teaspoonfuls of remaining cake mixture. Sprinkle with walnuts -- press lightly into the top. Bake for 350 degrees for 20 minutes. Cool slightly; cut into bars.

Chocolate Caramel Shortbread

1 1/2 c Butter, softened, divided 1/2 c Sifted icing sugar
1/4 ts Salt
1 1/4 c All purpose flour

1 cn Sweetened condensed milk
3 tb Corn syrup
1 ts Nanilla
3 Squares semi sweet chocolate, melted
Preheat oven to 350 degrees F. In large mixer bowl, beat 1 cup butter, sugar and salt until fluffy. Add flour, mix well. With floured finger, press evenly into greased 9 inch square pan. Bake 30-35 minutes or until lightly browned. Cool slightly. In 2 quart glass measure, with handle,in microwave oven, melt remaining 1/2 cup butter on high. for 1 minutes. Stir in sweetened condensed milk and corn syrup. Microwave on high for 6-8 minutes, stirring after each minute, or until mixture turns a light caramel color. Stir in vanilla. Spread over warm shortbread. Drizzle with chocolate. Chill until firm. Cut into bars. Store covered at room temperature. Makes 24 bars.

Chocolate Cheese Bars

1 Devil's Food Cake Mix (with or without pudding in it) 8 oz Cream cheese, softened
1/3 c Oil
3 Eggs (divided use)

1/4 c Sugar
6 oz Semi-sweet chocolate chips
1/2 c Walnuts or pecans, chopped
Mix dry cake mix, 2 eggs, and 1/3 cup oil until crumbly; reserve 1 cup. Pat remaining mixture lightly in an ungreased 13x9x2 inch pan. Bake for 15 minutes at 350 degrees. Remove and sprinkle top with chocolate chips and walnuts.
Beat cream cheese, sugar and remaining egg until light and smooth. Spread over chocolate chips and walnuts. Sprinkle with reserved crumb mixture. Return to oven and bake for 15 minutes longer. Cool and cut into bars. Makes 16 servings.

Chocolate Cherry Bars

1 pk Fudge cake mix
1 cn (21 oz.) cherry pie filling
1 ts Almond extract
2 Eggs; beaten
Frosting: 1 cup sugar 5 Tablespoons butter or margarine 1/3 cup milk 6 ounces semi-sweet chocolate chips
Preheat oven to 350. Grease and flour a 9x13 inch pan. Combine all ingredients for bars in a mixing bowl and stir by hand until mixed. Spread batter in prepared pan and bake 25-30 minutes. Be careful not to over-bake. Cool on rack.
To make frosting, combine sugar, butter and milk in small saucepan. Boil, stirring constantly, for 1 minute. Remove from heat, add chocolate pieces and stir until smooth. Pour over cooled bars.

Chocolate Chip Bars

3/4 c Brown Sugar firmly packed 1/2 c Butter or margarine
1 Egg
1 1/4 c All-purpose flour

1/2 ts Baking soda
1/2 ts Salt
1 ts Nanilla
6 oz Chocolate pieces
1/2 c Chopped walnuts

Cream together sugar and butter. Beat in egg. Stir in dry ingredients; add vanilla and mix. Fold in chocolate and nuts. Spread in greased 15 x 10-inch pan (this will be a thin layer of batter). Bake in 375 degree oven 12 to 15 minutes. Cool slightly before cutting into 48 squares.

Chocolate Chip Cookie Bars

3/4 c Firmly packed brown sugar 1/2 c Sugar
1/2 c Margarine or butter,softened 1/2 c Shortening

1 1/2 ts Nanilla
1 Egg
1 3/4 c All purpose flour
1 ts Baking soda
1/2 ts Salt
1 c Semi-sweet chocolate chips
1/2 c Chopped nuts or shelled
Sunflower seeds (opt)
Heat oven to 375 degrees F. In large bowl, combine brown sugar, sugar, margarine and shortening; beat until light and fluffy. Add vanilla and egg; blend well. Stir in flour, baking soda, and salt; mix well. Stir in chocolate chips and nuts. Spread in ungreased 13 x 9-inch pan. Bake for 15 to 25 minutes or until light golden brown. Cool completely. Cut into bars.

Chocolate Chip Cranberry Cheese Bars

1 c Butter or margarine, (2 sticks or 1/2 LB) 1 c Brown sugar; packed
2 c Flour
1 1/2 c Rolled oats

2 ts Orange zest; grated
1 pk Semisweet chocolate chips, 12oz
1 c Cranberries; dried (4oz)
1 pk Cream cheese; (8oz)
1 1/4 c Sweetened condensed milk, (1 can at 14oz)

Beat butter and brown sugar in large bowl until creamy; beat in flour, oats and orange peel until crumbly. Stir in chocolate chips and cranberries; reserve 2 cups mixture. Press remaining mixture onto bottom of greased 13-by-9-inch baking pan. Bake at 350 degrees 15 minutes.

Beat cream cheese in small bowl until smooth. Gradually beat in sweetened condensed milk. Pour over hot crust; sprinkle with reserved oat mixture. Return to oven and bake 25 to 30 minutes or until center is set. Cool in pan on wire rack.

Makes about 3 dozen.

Chocolate Chip Nut Bars

1/2 c Margarine
2 c Brown sugar, packed
1 ts Nanilla
2 Eggs
1 1/2 c Flour
2 ts Baking powder
1 ts Salt
1 c Chipits
1 c Nuts

Melt margarine in large pot. Remove from heat and add sugar and vanilla. Stir well. Add eggs, one at a time. Stir together flour, baking powder, and salt. Add to pan and mix well. Spread in pan 9X13. Sprinkle with nuts and chipits over surface and press down lightly. Bake at 350 for 35-40 minutes. Cool and cut into bars.

Chocolate Crunch Bars

1/2 c Honey
1/3 c Margarine
1/4 c Cocoa Powder, Sweetened --
1 c Granola
1 c Dry Milk
Blend together everything except the granola to a stiff dough. Knead in the granola, or roll the shaped bars in granola.
* Carob powder may be used also.

Chocolate Delight Bars

1/2 c Margarine -- softened 1 Egg yolk
2 tb Water
1 1/4 c Flour

1 ts Sugar
1 ts Baking powder
12 oz Chocolate chips
3/4 c Sugar
2 Eggs
6 tb Margarine -- melted
2 ts Nanilla
1 c 2c nuts -- chopped fine
Combine the first six ingredients and mix till smooth. Mixture will be very stiff. Press into a greased 9"x13" pan. Bake 10 minutes at 350 degrees F. Remove from oven and sprinkle with chocolate chips. Return to oven for 1 minute. Spread melted chips over the crust. Beat eggs till thick, then beat in sugar. Stir in melted margarine, vanilla and nuts. Spread over chocolate. Bake 30-35 minutes at 350 degrees F. Cut into 48 squares when cool.

Chocolate Fudge Bars

1 Stick Butter
2 oz Unsweetened Baking Chocolate Squares
1 c Sugar
2 Eggs
1 c Flour
1/2 ts Salt
1/2 ts Baking Soda
1/2 ts Nanilla Or Peppermint Extract
1 c Chocolate Chips
Glaze
1 c Powdered Sugar
1 tb Milk -- or more
1/2 ts Peppermint Extract
Melt the butter and the unsweetened chocolate.
When the bowl is cool, add the sugar, beat in the eggs, mix in the flour, the salt,
and the baking soda. Add the vanilla. Spread into a greased jellyroll pan.
Sprinkle with the chocolate chips, and bake at 350 F for 8 minutes or so.
Glaze: Mix up the ingredients. It should be like a glaze that will pour, thickly. Add
a couple of drops of food coloring if desired. When the cookies come out of the
oven, spread the glaze. Cool slightly, and cut while still warm.

Chocolate Maple Nut Bars

1 1/2 c Flour; unsifted
2/3 c Sugar
1/2 ts Salt
3/4 c Margarine or butter; cold 2 Eggs

14 oz Sweetened condensed milk
1 1/2 ts Maple flavoring
2 c Nuts; chopped
1 c Semi-sweet chocolate chips
Preheat oven to 350 degrees F. In a large bowl, combine flour, sugar and salt; cut in margarine until crumbly. stir in 1 beaten egg. Press evenly in a 9x13" pan. Bake for 25 minutes. Meanwhile, in medium bowl, beat sweetened condensed milk, remaining egg and flavoring; stir in nuts. Sprinkle chocolate chips evenly over the prepared crust. Top with the nut mixture. Bake for 25 minutes more or until lightly brown. Cool. Cut into bars. Store tightly covered at room temperature. Makes 24 - 36 bars.

Chocolate Marshmallow Bars

2 oz Unsweetened chocolate 1/2 c Butter
1 c Sugar
2 Eggs

1/2 c Flour
1 ts Nanilla
1 c Chopped pecans
16 Large marshmallows
Preheat oven to 350 degrees F. Grease an 11 1/2 x 7 baking pan. Melt chocolate and butter in top of double boiler over hot water. Set aside. Cream sugar and eggs until light and fluffy. Add flour. Beat. Add melted chocolate and butter. Beat well. Mix in vanilla and pecans. Pour into prepared pan. Bake 18 minutes.
Remove from oven and cover with marshmallows. Return to oven and bake until marshmallows are lightly browned.
Cool slightly and cut into bars.

Chocolate Meringue Bars

1/2 c Margarine 1/2 c Sugar
1/2 c Brown sugar 2 Eggs -- separated 1 ts Nanilla

2 ts Baking powder 1 ts Baking soda 1/2 ts Salt
3 tb Milk -- or water 6 oz Chocolate chips 1 c Brown sugar

1/2 ts Nanilla
1/2 c Nuts -- , optional
Beat margarine, sugars, egg yolks, and 1 tsp. vanilla. Mix dry ingredients, and add with milk. Spread in 9"x13" pan. Sprinkle with chocolate chips. Beat egg whites to soft peaks, beat in brown sugar and vanilla. Fold in nuts. Spread carefully over chips. Bake 30-35 min. at 325 degrees F.

Chocolate Pecan Cheesecake Bars

Crust:
1 pk Chocolate cake mix
1/2 c Butter or margarine -- Softened
1 Egg
1/2 c Pecans -- chopped
Filling:
8 oz Cream cheese -- softened
14 oz Sweetened condensed milk
1 ts Nanilla
1 Egg
Heat oven to 350. Grease 13 x 9 pan. In large bowl, combine cake mix, margarine and egg; mix at low speed until combined. Stir in pecans. Reserve 1 cup for topping; set aside. Press remaining mixture evenly in bottom of greased pan. Beat cream cheese in medium bowl until fluffy. Add remaining filling ingredients and beat at medium speed until smooth. Pour over crust; sprinkle with reserved topping. Bake at 350 for 35 to 40 minutes. Cool completely. Cut into bars. Store in refrigerator.

Chocolate Raisin Bars

1 3/4 c All-purpose flour 1 pn Salt
8 ts Potato flour
3/4 c Butter

1/3 c Raisins; chopped
8 oz Semisweet chocolate pieces
1/4 c Nanilla sugar
Preheat oven to 350 F (175 C). Sift all-purpose flour, salt, potato flour and vanilla sugar into a medium-size bowl. Cut in butter until mixture forms coarse crumbs; mix in raisins. Mix together to form a soft dough. Roll out dough on a floured surface to a rectangle slightly smaller than an 11" x 7" baking pan. Place rolled-out dough in pan; press to fit. Smooth top; prick well. Bake about 25 minutes or until very lightly browned. Cool a few minutes. Using a sharp knife, mark through surface of mixture with lines to use as a guide for cutting. Let cool in pan. Cut mixture in 20 squares; remove from pan. Place chocolate in a small bowl over a pan of gently simmering water; stir until melted and smooth. Line a baking sheet with foil. Dip bars in chocolate, coating evenly; lift out with a fork and tap gently on side of bowl to remove excess chocolate. Place on foil. Place baking sheet in a cool place until chocolate sets. If desired, any remaining chocolate can be piped over bars for decoration.

Chocolate Raspberry Bars

1 1/2 c Rolled oats
1/2 c Unbleached flour
1/2 c Almonds, ground
pn Salt
1 ts Ground cinnamon
1/3 c Tiny semi-sweet chocolate chips
2 Eggs
1/2 c Maple syrup
1/2 c All-fruit raspberry jam

In a medium bowl, combine the oats, flour, almonds, salt, cinnamon and chocolate chips.

Combine the eggs and maple syrup in a small bowl and whisk until very well combined. Pour into the oat mixture and combine well. About halfway through the mixing it will become much easier if you use your hands.

Scoop half of the dough into the bottom of a 9-inch glass pie dish and smooth it out, going up the side a little bit, to make a smooth layer. If the dough is too sticky to work with, wet your hands and use them to press it in.

Spread the jam evenly over the dough in the pie dish. Then use your hands to very gently distribute the remaining dough over the the jam. In some places the jam might squish up over the top of this new layer of dough, but that is OK.

Microcook, uncovered, at full power (100%) until the dough feels dry to the touch, about 5 minutes. The raspberry jam will be bubbly and very runny, but let it cool completely before cutting into bars and it will be fine.

Makes 12 bars.

Chocolate Walnut Bars

Crust:
1 1/2 c Flour 1/2 c Margarine 1/4 c Brown sugar 3/4 c Corn syrup 2 tb Margarine; melted 1 ts Nanilla 12 oz Chocolate chips
Filling:
3 Eggs 3/4 c Sugar 1 1/2 c Walnuts; chopped
For crust, beat flour, margarine and brown sugar in small mixer bowl until crumbly. Press into greased 13 x 9 pan. Bake in preheated 350 oven for 12 to 15 minutes. For filling, beat eggs, sugar, corn syrup, margarine and vanilla in medium bowl with wire whisk. Stir in morsels and walnuts. Pour over crust. Bake in preheated oven for 25 to 30 minutes or until set. Chill for a few minutes before cutting.

Chocolaty Poppers

1/2 c Land O'Lakes Butter
10 1/2 oz Marshmallows, miniature
2 oz Semi sweet chocolate
1 c All purpose flour
1 ts Nanilla extract
1 c Salted peanuts
6 c Popcorn
Combine butter, marshmallows and chocolate in a 2 quart saucepan. Cook over low heat, stirring constantly, until melted and well blended. Remove from heat. Gradually add flour and salt, mixing well. Stir in vanilla and peanuts. Pour over popcorn, mixing well. Press into well greased 13x9 inch pan. Bake at 350 degrees for 10 to 12 minutes. Cool; cut into bars. Dust with confectioners sugar, if desired.

Congo Bars

2 3/4 c Unbleached All-Purpose Flour 2 1/2 ts Baking Powder
1/2 ts Salt
3 lg Eggs

2 c Brown Sugar, Firmly Packed
1 ts Nanilla
2/3 c Negetable Oil
6 oz Chocolate Chips, 1 Cup
Sift the flour, baking powder and salt together, blending well. In a separate bowl, beat the eggs. Add the sugar, vanilla and oil. Stir in the dry ingredients, then add the chocolate chips. Spread on a greased jelly-roll pan and bake for 15 to 20 minutes in a preheated 350 Degree F. oven. Cool slightly before cutting.

Crunchy Chocolate Peanut Butter Bars

1/2 c Light corn syrup
1/3 c Brown sugar, packed
1 c Peanut butter
3 c Rice cereal
1 c Semi-sweet chocolate pieces
2 ts Nanilla

In a 2 quart saucepan, combine corn syrup and brown sugar,. Cook and stir till mixture comes to a full boil. Stir in peanut butter. Remove from heat. Stir in cereal, chocolate pieces and vanilla. Stir in cereal, chocolate pieces and vanilla. Press into an ungreased 9x9x2 inch pan. Chill 1 hour. Cut into bars.

Deluxe Chocolate Marshmallow Bars

3/4 c Butter or margarine 1 1/2 c Sugar
3 Eggs
1 ts Nanilla extract

1 1/3 c All-purpose flour 1/2 ts Baking powder 1/2 ts Salt
3 tb Baking cocoa

1/2 c Chopped nuts, optional 4 c Miniature marshmallows Topping:
1 1/3 c Chocolate chips (8 oz.) 3 tb Butter or margarine

1 c Peanut butter
2 c Crisp rice cereal

In a mixing bowl, cream butter and sugar. Add eggs and vanilla; beat until fluffy. Combine flour, baking powder, salt and cocoa; add to creamed mixture. Stir in nuts if desired. Spread in a greased jelly roll pan. Bake at 350 for 15-18 minutes. Sprinkle marshmallows evenly over cake; return to oven for 2-3 minutes. Using a knife dipped in water, spread the melted marshmallows evenly over cake. Cool. For topping, combine chocolate chips, butter and peanut butter in a small saucepan. Cook over low heat, stirring constantly, until melted and well blended. Remove from heat, stir in cereal. Spread over bars. Chill.

Easy Chocolate Chip Layer Bars

1 Stick butter or margarine
1 1/2 c Graham cracker crumbs
1 c Flaked coconut (opt)
12 oz Semi sweet chocolate morsels
14 oz Can sweetened condensed milk
1 c Chopped pecans
Preheat oven to 350 degrees. Melt butter in oven in 13x9 inch baking pan.
Remove from oven. Sprinkle crumbs over butter. Sprinkle with coconut and
morsels. Pour sweetened condensed milk evenly over mixture. Top with pecans;
press down.
Bake for 22 - 27 minutes or until golden brown around edges. Cool completely in
pan on rack.

Fundy Mud Bars

1 c Margarine
2 c Sugar
4 Eggs
1 1/2 c All purpose flour 1/3 c Cocoa

1 c Chopped walnuts
3 c Miniature Marshmallows
1/2 c Margarine
4 c Icing sugar
1/3 c Cocoa
1/2 c Evaporated milk

Cream margarine and sugar until light and fluffy. Add eggs, one at a time, beating well after each addition. Sift cocoa and flour together, beat in gradually. Stir in walnuts. Spoon batter into a greased 9 x13 inch pan. Bake at 350 degrees F oven for 30 - 35 minutes. Immediately sprinkle top of cake with marshmallows. Return to oven for 3 - 5 minutes until marshmallows are slightly puffed. Cool 30 minutes. For icing, cream margarine. Combine icing sugar and cocoa, and beat in alternately with milk. Beat until icing is light and fluffy. Spread over marshmallow layer. Chill to serve - cut in bars.

Oatmeal Chocolate Chip Bars

1 1/2 c Brown sugar, packed 1 c Shortening
2 tb Molasses
2 ts Nanilla

2 Whole egg
3 c Rolled oats
1 c Flour
1 ts Baking soda
1 ts Salt
3/4 c Nuts -- chopped
12 oz Semisweet chocolate chips
Preheat oven to 350 degrees. Grease 15 x 10 or 13 x 9 inch pan. In large bowl, beat brown sugar and shortening until light and fluffy. Add molasses, vanilla, and eggs; blend well. Lightly spoon flour into measuring cup; level off. Stir in oats, flour, baking soda and salt; blend well. Stir in nuts and chocolate chips. Spread in prepared pan. Bake at 350 degrees for 20 to 25 minutes or until light golden brown and center is set. Cool slightly; cut into bars. Serve warm or cool. 48 bars.

Peanut Butter Bars

3/4 c Butter
2 c Peanut butter
1 1/2 c Crushed graham crackers
1 lb Powdered sugar
6 oz Chocolate chips
1 tb Crisco oil
Mix first 4 ingredients - knead until smooth. Press into 9 x 13" pan. Melt chocolate chips in saucepan with oil. Spread over mixture in pan. Chill 1 hour & cut into bars.

Reese's Bars

1 c Melted butter
2 3/4 c Icing sugar
1 c Peanut butter
2 1/2 c Graham wafer crumbs
12 oz Chocolate chips
Mix together first four and press into an ungreased 9 x 13 pan.
Melt the chocolate chips and pour over the peanut butter mixture. Let cool
slightly and then cut into bars before the chocolate hardens completely.

Scrumptious Chocolate Layer Bars

Filling:
12 oz Chocolate chips
5 oz Can evaporated milk
8 oz Cream cheese
1/2 ts Almond extract
Crust:
3 c Flour
1 c Butter, softened
2 Eggs
1 ts Baking powder
1/2 ts Almond extract

Mix chocolate chips, cream cheese and evaporated milk in a saucepan. Cook over low heat, stirring constantly, until mixture is smooth. Remove from heat and stir in 1/2 tsp. almond extract. Mix well;set aside. Combine remaining ingredients. Blend well until mixture resembles coarse crumbs. Press 1/2 crumbs (not too hard) in greased 9 x 13 pan. Spread with chocolate mixture. Sprinkle remaining 1/2 of crumbs over filling. Bake at 375 degrees F for 35-40 minutes or until golden brown. Cool and cut into bars. Makes approx. 36 bars.

Snicker Bars

11 1/2 oz Milk chocolate chips 2 tb Shortening
30 Nanilla caramels
2 tb Water

1 c Chopped peanuts
Melt chips and shortening in microwave. Stir until smooth. Pour 1/2 of chocolate mixture into 8" foil lined pan. Refrigerate until firm (about 15 minutes). Put caramels, butter and water in bowl and heat in microwave. Stir until smooth. Blend in nuts. Pour over first chocolate mixture; refrigerate until tacky (about 15 minutes). Reheat remaining chocolate. if necessary, pour over top, chill, cut and enjoy.

Thin Fudgy Chocolate Strippers

1 1/2 c All-purpose flour
1/3 Cap unsweetened cocoa
1/2 ts Baking soda
1/4 ts Salt
1 c Sugar
3 tb Stick margarine, softened
1 ts Instant espresso granules Or 2 ts Instant coffee granules
1 ts Nanilla extract
1 (2 1/2-ounce) jar prune baby food
1 lg Egg
Nonstick cooking spray
1 (1-oz) square semisweet chocolate, chopped
1 (1-oz) square white baking chocolate, chopped

Preheat oven 350 F. Mix flour, cocoa, baking soda and salt in bowl; stir well. Combine sugar, margarine, espresso, vanilla, baby food and egg in large bowl. Beat at high speed with mixer for 2 minutes; stir in dry ingredients (dough will be thick). Spoon dough into 15xlO-inch jellyroll pan coated with cooking spray. Bake 13 minutes. (Do not overcook.) Cool completely in pan. Cut into 36 bars. Place bars on wax paper. Place semisweet chocolate in heavy duty zip-top plastic bag; place white chocolate in a heavy-duty Tiptop plastic bag. Microwave both bags at Medium-Low (30 percent power) for 1 minute or until chocolate melts. Knead bags until smooth. Snip a tiny hole in corner of each bag; drizzle chocolates over bars. Allow drizzle on bars to cool, before eating. Makes 3 dozen. Note: Can be made ahead of time, and stored in airtight container. Drizzle chocolates onto bars on the day you wish to serve them.

Balls

Coconut fudge balls

2/3 c. evaporated milk
2 1/2 c. powdered sugar
12 oz. semi sweet chocolate bits 1 c. chopped nuts
7 oz. or more coconut

Mix chocolate bits and milk and microwave until melted (about 3 minutes).
Stir in sugar, and nuts. Chill 1/2 hour. Roll into balls. Color coconut and roll balls
in the coconut.

Fudge Rum Balls

1 pkg. Duncan Hines Moist Deluxe Butter Recipe Fudge Cake Mix 1 c. finely chopped pecans or walnuts
1 tbsp. rum extract
2 c. sifted confectioners' sugar

1/4 c. unsweetened cocoa
Pecans or walnuts, finely chopped

1. Preheat oven to 375 degrees F. Grease and flour 13x9x2 inch pan. Prepare, bake and cool cake following package directions.
2. Crumble cake into large bowl. Stir with fork until crumbs are fine and uniform in size. Add 1 cup nuts, rum extract, confectioners' sugar and cocoa. Stir until well blended.

3. Shape heaping tablespoonfuls mixture into balls. Garnish by rolling balls in finely chopped nuts. Press firmly to adhere nuts to balls. Makes 6 dozen. Tip: Substitute real rum for rum extract.

Cappuccino Bon-Bons

1 package family-size brownie mix (13 x 9) size 2 eggs
1/3 cup of water
1/3 cup cooking oil

1 1/2 tbsp. instant coffee
1 tsp. ground cinnamon
Whipped topping
Small or large foil cupcake liners
Preheat oven to 350 degrees
Place foil cupcake liners on cookie sheet Combine all ingredients except Whip
Cream Fill small liners with 1 tbsp. of filling

Fill large liners with 1/4 cup of mix.
Bake small cupcakes 12-15 minutes.
Bake large 20-25 minutes, or until toothpick comes out clean.
Cool completely.
Garnish with a dollop of whip cream and a sprinkle of cinnamon before serving.

Chocolate Filled Bon Bons

1/2 c. butter flavor shortening 1/2 c. granulated sugar
1/4 c. firmly packed brown sugar 1 tsp. vanilla

1 egg
1 2/3 all purpose flour, unsifted 36 chocolate kisses
36 peach halves

Cream shortening, sugars, vanilla and egg in large bowl at medium speed of mixer. Combine flour, baking soda, and salt. Stir into creamed mixture. Press 2 level measuring teaspoonfuls dough around each kiss, covering kiss completely. Gently place pecan half on top of each. Bake on ungreased baking sheet for 6-7 minutes (cookies will not brown, do not over bake). Gently press pecans into hot cookies. Cool on baking sheet for 1 minute, then remove to cooling racks.

Chocolate Brittle

1 LB Sugar
1 LB Walnuts, finely chopped 1 LB Almonds
1 LB Semi Sweet Chocolate 1 LB Whole Walnuts

In a saucepan cook butter and sugar, boiling 5 minutes. Stir in almonds and cook 10-20 minutes or until nuts begin to pop and turn brown. Pour into a shallow pan and let cool. Melt chocolate and pour over mixture in pan. Sprinkle w/ finely chopped walnuts. After mixture hardens, turn over and sprinkle bottom w/ walnuts. Break Candy into pieces.

1 prepared 9-inch pie shell, baked

Carob Candy Balls

1/2 c Carob powder
1/2 c Honey
1/2 c Peanut butter
1/2 c Sesame seeds
1/4 c Wheat germ
1/4 c Dry milk powder
1 c Honey graham cracker crumbs

Blend together carob powder, honey, peanut butter, sesame seeds, wheat germ and powdered milk. Form into 1 1/2-inch balls. Roll in graham cracker crumbs. Refrigerate 1 hour before serving. This candy is low in salt, high in potassium.
Makes 24 candy balls

Chocolate Balls

2 Sticks margarine
1 1/2 c Graham cracker crumbs
1/2 c Chopped pecans
1 c Coconut
1 Box powdered sugar
1 tb Nanilla
12 oz Jar crunchy peanut butter
6 oz Package semisweet chocolate chips
1/2 Cake paraffin wax (half of 1/4 pound size)
Melt margarine in large container. Stir in graham cracker crumbs, pecans, coconut, powdered sugar and vanilla; add peanut butter and mix well. Roll into walnut size balls and lay out on waxed paper. Melt chocolate and paraffin together over hot water. Using 2 teaspoons (or any method you prefer) dip each ball into mixture returning to waxed paper. The balls will cool quickly. Yield 6 dozen.

Chocolate Bourbon Balls

1/2 c Margarine or butter 4 c Powdered sugar
1 c Finely chopped nuts 1/4 c Bourbon

1 pk (6 ounces) milk chocolate chips
3 tb Half-and-half.
Place margarine in medium bowl. Microwave at HIGH (100%) until melted, 1 to 2 minutes. Mix in sugar, nuts and bourbon. Refrigerate until firm.
Shape into 1-inch balls. Refrigerate until firm. Combine chocolate chips and half-and-half in a small bowl. Microwave at MEDIUM-HIGH (70%) until chocolate chips are melted, 1 to 2-1/2 minutes, stirring once or twice. Stir until smooth. Drizzle chocolate over candies. (Reheat chocolate as needed.) Chill.

Chocolate Cream Hazelnut Balls

1/2 c Finely chopped hazelnuts 1 c Nanilla cookie crumbs
1 c Powdered sugar
2 tb Cocoa

2 tb Corn syrup
1/4 c Cream
1/2 ts Nanilla
Combine all ingredients and mix well. The mixture should be moist to the touch.
Roll into balls about the size of a walnut. Roll in powdered sugar or finely
chopped hazelnuts. Store for at least 2 days in covered container.

Chocolate Mint Dessert Balls

9 oz Chocolate chips; melted 1/2 c Creme de menthe
24 oz Cream cheese; softened 1 ts Cinnamon, ground

2 c Pecans; finely chopped
Chocolate cookie wafers
In large bowl, mix together ingredients except pecans until smooth. cover and chill 1 hour. Divide mixture into 1 part per ball, and form into balls. Roll balls in pecans. Serve with chocolate cookie wafers. Store in refrigerator.

Chocolate Pecan Rum Balls

1 lb Pecans, shelled and ground
8 1/2 oz Chocolate wafers; crushed
1/2 c Dark rum
1/3 c Honey
Powdered sugar
Combine all ingredients, except powdered sugar, in a large bowl. Mix well. Chill for 20 minutes. Shape by spoonful into round balls. Store in a tightly covered, airtight container. Just before serving or giving, roll in powdered sugar. Makes 100 balls.

Chocolate Walnut Rum Balls

1 c Walnuts, ground or finely chopped
2 c Grated "German's sweet" or bittersweet chocolate
1 1/2 c Sifted confectioner's sugar
4 tb Rum
Cocoa powder
Combine nuts, sugar, and chocolate. Moisten with rum to form a stiff dough.
Form into small balls and roll in cocoa to coat.

Dietetic Cream Cheese Balls

1 pk (8 0z. size) cream cheese
3/4 c Finely chopped pecans
Milkcote or whitecoat chocolate
Cream the cream cheese and add pecans. Chill until cheese will form balls. Dip
balls into melted whitecote or milkcote chocolate coating. Makes about 25 balls.

Double Chocolate Cherry Bourbon Balls

1 6oz.pkg. chocolate chips
3 T Corn syrup
1/2 c Bourbon or 1/4 cup bourbon and 1/4 cup ginger ale
1 8 1/2 oz.pkg. chocolate wafers, crushed
1/2 c Confectioners sugar
1 c Finely chopped nuts
1/4 c Finely chopped candied cherries
Granulated sugar
Melt chocolate in top of double boiler. Remove from heat, add corn syrup and bourbon. In large bowl mix wafer crumbs, nuts, confectioners sugar and cherries. Add chocolate mixture. Stir until blended. Refrigerate 1 hour. Roll into 1-inch balls and roll in granulated sugar.

Swedish Balls

1/2 lb Butter
1 1/2 c Sugar
2 Eggs
1/2 c Strong cold coffee (instant) 2 ts Nanilla

1 c Cocoa
4 c Quick-cooking oats, uncooked
Cream butter and sugar. Blend in eggs. Add coffee, vanilla, and cocoa. Mix. Add oats and mix well. Chill 1 to 2 hours. Shape into one-inch balls. Roll in sugar. Store in air tight container. Keep refrigerated. Makes 5 dozen.

Sweet 'n' Peanutty Chocolate Balls

3 c Powdered sugar, sifted
1 1/2 c Graham cracker crumbs
1 c Pecans finely chopped
3/4 c Butter
3/4 c Peanut butter
1 1/2 c Semisweet chocolate chips
4 tb Butter
1 tb Milk

Combine powdered sugar, graham cracker crumbs and pecans; stir until uniform in color. In a saucepan, melt butter and peanut butter together. Pour over sugar mix, and stir until just moistened. Form into one-inch balls. In a separate saucepan, combine chocolate chips, butter and milk. Melt together over low heat, stirring just enough to blend. Coat balls with chocolate by dipping into chocolate mixture one at a time. Place on waxed paper, and chill before serving. Makes 60 balls

Walnut Chocolate Rum Balls

1 c Walnuts, ground or finely chopped
2 c Grated "German's sweet" or bittersweet chocolate
1 1/2 c Sifted confectioner's sugar
4 tb Rum
Cocoa powder

Combine nuts, sugar, and chocolate. Moisten with rum to form a stiff dough. Form into small balls and roll in cocoa to coat. This recipe is not only simple, it's flexible. It can be made with other kinds of liquor (amaretto, sherry, and Southern Comfort work well), nuts (almonds or pecans, for instance) and coatings (ground nuts, finely grated coconut, etc.) and always comes out tasting great. Adding small chunks of nut for texture is also effective.

Biscotti

Chocolate Almond Biscotti

1/2 c Butter or margarine softened 1 1/4 c Sugar
2 Eggs
1 ts Almond extract

2 1/4 c All-purpose flour
1/4 c Hershey's Cocoa -OR- European Style Cocoa
1 ts Baking powder
1/4 ts Salt
1 c Sliced almonds
Additional sliced almonds (optional)
Chocolate Glaze:
1 c Hershey's Semi-Sweet Chips
1 tb Shortening*
White Glaze:
1/4 c Premier White Chips (Hershey's)
1 ts Shortening
*(do not use butter, margarine or oil in Glaze recipes).
Heat oven to 350 degrees F. In large bowl, beat butter and sugar until well blended. Add eggs and almond extract; beat until smooth. Stir together flour, cocoa, baking powder and salt; blend into butter mixture, beating until smooth. (Dough will be thick.) Using wooden spoon, work almonds into dough. Divide dough in half. With lightly floured hands, shape each half into rectangular log about 2 inches in diameter and 11 inches long; place on large ungr eased cookie sheet, at least 2 inches apart. Bake 30 minutes or until logs are set. Remove from oven; cool on cookie sheet 15 minutes. Using serrated knife and sawing motion, cut logs into 1/2-inch diagonal slices. Discard end pieces. Arrange slices, cut sides down, close together on cookie sheet. Bake 8 to 9 minutes. Turn each slice over; bake an additional 8 to 9 minutes. Remove from oven; cool on cookie sheet on wire rack. Dip end of each biscotti in Chocolate Glaze or drizzle glaze over entire cookie. Drizzle White Glaze over chocolate glaze. Garnish with additional almonds, if desired. About 2-1/2 dozen cookies.
Chocolate Glaze: In small microwave-safe bowl, place 1 cup Hershey's Semi-Sweet Chocolate Chips and 1 tablespoon shortening (do not use butter, margarine or oil). Microwave at HIGH (100%) 1 to 1-1/2

minutes or until smooth when stirred. About 1 cup glaze.
White Glaze: In small microwave-safe bowl, place 1/4 cup Hershey's Premier White Chips and 1 teaspoon shortening (do not use butter, margarine or oil). Microwave at HIGH (100%) 30 to 45 seconds or until smooth when stirred. About 1/4 cup glaze.

Chocolate Biscotti

4 oz Unsweetened chocolate 1/2 c Butter
1/2 ts Nanilla extract
3 lg Eggs

1 1/4 c Sugar
3 c All-purpose flour
1/2 ts Baking powder
1 c Hazelnuts or walnuts; chop
1 Egg white; lightly beaten
Melt chocolate and butter in a heavy saucepan over low heat. Beat eggs at medium speed with an electric mixer until frothy; gradually add sugar, beating until thick and pale (about 5 minutes). Add chocolate mixture, stirring until blended. Combine flour and baking powder; stir into chocolate mixture. Stir in nuts. Flour hands, and form dough into a 13" log. Place on a lightly greased baking sheet. Brush with egg white. Bake at 350F for 45 minutes; cool on a wire rack. Cut log with a serrated knife crosswise into 24 (1/2-inch) slices, and place on an ungreased cookie sheet. Bake at 350F for 10 minutes on each side. Remove to wire racks to cool.

Chocolate Peanut Biscotti

2 1/4 c All-Purpose Flour
2 1/4 ts Baking powder
1/3 c Butter, room temperature
2/3 c Granulated sugar
3 lg Eggs, room temperature
1/2 c (3 oz) semisweet-chocolate chips, melted
1 ts Nanilla extract
3/4 c Unsalted dry roasted peanuts, chopped
1/2 c Mini-size M&M's candies
White from 1 lg egg
Mix flour and baking powder.
Beat butter and sugar in a large bowl with electric mixer until blended. Beat in eggs, then melted chocolate and vanilla. Stir in flour mixture, peanuts and mini-size candies.
Divide dough in half (2 cups per half). Wrap in plastic wrap and refrigerate 3 hours or until firm enough to handle.
Heat oven to 350 degrees F. Lightly grease one large cookie sheet. With a fork, lightly beat egg white in a small bowl.
Put both pieces off dough on cookie sheet, about 4 inches apart. With floured hands, shape into 14x1 1/2-inch logs. Brush with egg white. Bake 25 to 30 minutes until firm when pressed in center. (Tops may crack slightly.) Remove cookie sheet from oven to a wire rack. (Leave oven on.) Let logs cool 10 minutes, then slide them onto a cutting board. With a large serrated knife, cut each log diagonally in 30 slices. Lay slices on ungreased cookie sheets. Bake 8 to 10 minutes longer, turning once, until dry and lightly toasted. Cool completely on cookie sheets on wire rack. Store airtight up to 1 month or freeze.
Prep: 20 min. Chill: 3 hr. Bake: 40 min.

Chocolate Nanilla Chip Biscotti

2 1/2 c All-purpose flour
1/3 c Unsweetened cocoa powder
3 ts Baking powder
1/2 c Sugar
1/2 c Brown sugar; packed
1/4 c Margarine or butter; softened
3 Eggs
1 c White vanilla chips

Heat oven to 350 degrees F Spray 1 large or 2 small cookie sheets with nonstick cooking spray. Lightly spoon flour into measuring cup; level off. In med bowl, combine flour, cocoa and baking powder; mix well. In large bowl, combine sugar, brown sugar and margarine; beat well. Add flour mixture; mix well. Stir in white vanilla chops. With spray coated hands, firmly shape dough into 3 rolls, about 7 inches long. Place rolls at least 3 inches apart on sprayed cookie sheet; flatten each to form 3/4 inch thick rectangle, about 3 inches wide and 7 inches long. Bake at 350 degrees F for 22-28 min or until rectangles are light golden brown and centers are firm to the touch. Place rectangles on wire racks; cool 5 min. Wipe cookie sheet clean. With serrated knife, cut each rectangle into 1/2 inch slices; place, cut side up, on cookie sheet. Bake at 350 degrees F for 6-8 min or until top surface is slightly dry. Turn cookies over; bake an additional 6-8 min or until top surface is slightly dry. Remove cookies from cookie sheets; cool completely on wire racks. Store tightly covered.

Chocolate Walnut Biscotti

2 c Walnut Halves (about 8 oz) 3 oz Unsweetened chocolate
5 tb Unsalted butter plus
1 ts Unsalted butter

2 c Flour
2 ts Baking powder
3 Eggs
1 c Sugar
1 ts Grated orange zest

Preheat oven to 350 degrees. Place the walnuts on a cookie sheet and toast until golden brown, about 10 minutes. Let cool and then chop coarsely. In a double boiler over simmering water, melt the chocolate and butter together. Remove from the heat and stir until smooth. Let cool for 10 minutes.

Sift together the flour and baking powder. In a large bowl, beat the eggs lightly. Gradually beat in the sugar. Add the orange zest. Stir in the cooled chocolate until blended. Stir in the flour and baking powder until incorporated. Fold in the chopped walnuts. Divide the dough in half, wrap in plastic wrap and refrigerate at least 1 hour or overnight. Butter a large cookie sheet and preheat the oven to 350 degrees. Shape each half of the dough into a 14 x 2-1/2-inch log. Place about 4 inches apart on the prepared pan. Smooth the tops and sides with a rubber spatula. Bake for 40-45 minutes, or until the logs are firm when pressed in the center. Remove the baking sheet from the oven. Do not turn off the oven. Slide the logs onto a cutting board. With a large knife, cut each log diagonally into 1/2-inch slices. Stand the slices upright on edge on the prepared cookie sheet. Return to the oven and bake for 15 minutes longer, or until crisp. Transfer to wire racks to cool completely.

Chocolate-Chip Biscotti

1 1/4 c All-purpose flour
1/2 c Semisweet chocolate chips - Mini-morsels
1/3 c Sugar
3/4 ts Baking powder
1 tb Water
1 ts Nanilla extract
1 Egg
1 Egg white
Negetable cooking spray
Combine first 4 ingredients in a large bowl. Combine water and next 3
ingredients; add to flour mixture, stirring until well-blended (dough will be dry.)
Turn the dough out onto a lightly floured surface, and knead lightly 7 or 8 times.
Shape dough into a 16 inch long roll. Place roll on a baking sheet coated with
cooking spray, and flatten roll to 1 inch thickness. Bake at 350F for 25 minutes.
Remove roll from baking sheet to wire rack, and let cool 10 minutes. Cut roll
diagonally into 24 (1/2 inch) slices, and place, cut sides down, on baking sheet.
Reduce oven temp. to 325F, and bake 10 more minutes. Turn cookies over and
bake an additional 10 minutes (cookies will be slightly soft in center but will
harden as they cool.) Remove from baking sheet; let cool completely on wire
rack. Yield: 2 dozen (serving size: 1 cookie.)

Bread

American Chocolate Bread

1 1/2 c All-purpose flour or bread flour 1 c Warm water (105 - 115 F)
2 Envelopes dry yeast
2 tb Honey

Dough:
1 c Lukewarm milk (95 F)
3 tb Butter, melted
4 To 5 cups all-purpose flour or bread flour
8 oz Semisweet chocolate, coarsely chopped
1 Egg beaten with 2 Tbs whipping cream (glaze)
Sugar
Makes 8 small loaves
Sponge:
For sponge: Whisk flour, water, yeast and honey in large bowl until smooth.
cover with plastic. Let stand in warm draft-free area 1 hour. For dough: Stir down
sponge, using wooden spoon. Blend in milk, butter and salt. Mix in enough flour
1/2 cup at a time to form soft dough. Knead on floured surface until smooth and
no longer sticky, adding more flour if necessary, about 10 minutes.
Grease large bowl. Add dough, turning to coat entire surface. Cover bowl with
plastic. Let rise in warm draft-free area until doubled, about 1 1/4 hours.
Grease eight 2 1/2 x 4 1/2-inch loaf pans. Gently knead dough on lightly floured
surface until deflated. Pat out to 3/4 inch-thick rectangle. Cut into 8 even pieces.
Pat each out into 4x7-inch rectangle. Spread 1 ounce chocolate on short end of
each. Roll up jelly roll fashion. Pinch seam and ends to seal. Arrange seam side
down in prepared pans. Cover with kitchen towel. Let rise for 15 minutes to
lighten.
Preheat oven to 375 degrees F. Brush loaves with egg glaze and sprinkle with
sugar. Bake until light brown and loaves sound hollow when tapped on bottom,
about 30 minutes. Immediately remove from pans. Cool on racks 10 minutes.
Serve loaves hot.

Banana Chocolate Chip Bread

1/2 c Milk
1/2 c Nery ripe bananas; mashed
1 lg Egg
1 tb Butter or margarine
1 ts Salt
3 c Bread flour
1/3 c Semi sweet chocolate pieces
2 ts Bread machine yeast
Add ingredients in order given, adding mashed bananas with milk and chocolate with flour. Basic/white bread cycle. Light color setting.

Banana Nut Chocolate Chip Bread

1/3 c Butter or margarine, softened 3/4 c Sugar
1 ea Egg
1 c Mashed banana

2 c All purpose flour
2 1/2 ts Baking powder
1/4 ts Baking soda
1/2 ts Salt
1 c Chopped pecans (or walnuts)
1/2 c Chocolate chips (or more if desired
1/2 c Buttermilk
Preheat oven to 350 degrees F. Cream butter and sugar. Mix in egg and banana.
Stir together flour, baking powder, baking soda, salt, nuts and chocolate chips.
Add this mixture to creamed mixture alternately with buttermilk. Stir until just
blended. Pour batter into a greased and floured loaf pan (9 x 5 x 3 inches). Bake
for 65 minutes, or until bread tests done. Cool in pan for about 5 minutes, then
turn out on a wire rack. Makes 1 loaf.

Barley Bread

1 c Plus 2 tbsp water [80 degrees F.] 2 tb Honey
2 c All purpose flour
1 c Whole wheat flour

1/2 c Barley flour 1 ts Salt
2 ts Cocoa
1 ts Instant coffee 1 tb Butter

2 ts Active dry yeast
Add water and honey to the pan. Add flours, salt, cocoa and coffee to the pan.
Tap pan to settle the ingredients and level ingredients with your fingers or a
spatula. Place a piece of butter in each corner of the pan. Make a small well in
the flour and add the yeast. Program for whole wheat and a dark crust.

Chocolate Apple Bread

Topping:
1 tb Sugar
1/2 ts Cinnamon
1/2 c Chopped walnuts or pecans
Bread:
4 c All-purpose flour
1 ts Salt
1 ts Baking powder
1 ts Baking soda
1 ts Cinnamon
1/2 ts Nutmeg
1 c Butter,softened
2 c Sugar
4 Eggs
2 ts Nanilla extract
1/4 c Buttermilk
3 c Coarsely chopped apples
1 c Chopped walnuts
12 oz Semi-sweet chocolate chips

Topping: In cup, combine sugar, cinnamon and walnuts; set aside. Bread:
Preheat oven to 350 degrees F. Grease two 9x5x3" loaf pans. In small bowl,
combine flour, salt, baking powder, baking soda, cinnamon and nutmeg; set
aside. In large bowl, beat butter and sugar until creamy. Add eggs and vanilla
extract; mix well. Gradually beat in flour mixture alternately with buttermilk. Stir
in apples, walnuts, and chocolate chips. Pour into prepared pans. Sprinkle with
topping. 3. bake 50-60 minutes until cake tester inserted in center comes out
clean. Cool 15 minutes; remove from pans. Cool completely. Makes 2 loaves.

Chocolate Banana Bread

1 c Bananas; mashed 1 1/2 Eggs
3 tb Butter
1 1/2 ts Nanilla extract 1/4 ts Salt

1/2 ts Cinnamon
1 1/2 tb Unsweetened cocoa
3 tb Sugar
3 c Bread flour
2 ts Yeast
3 tb Chopped walnuts; optional
As with any bread which derives liquid from the fruit, watch the dough and add milk or water, if necessary, one Tablespoon at a time, until a nice round ball of dough is formed.

Chocolate Bunny Bread

3 1/4 -3 3/4 cups all-purpose flour 2/3 c Sugar
1/3 c Unsweetened coca powder
2 pk Rapid rise yeast

3/4 ts Salt
2/3 c Milk
1/4 c Water
1/4 c Butter/margarine 1 Egg

1 tb Pure vanilla extract
1/3 c Milk chocolate or peanut butter morsels
Decorations (optional) are Jelly beans, icing
In large bowl, combine 1 cup flour, sugar, cocoa powder, undissolved yeast and salt. Heat milk, water and butter until very warm (120-130 degrees). Gradually add to dry ingredients; beat 2 minutes at medium speed of electric mixer, scraping bowl occasionally. Add egg, vanilla and 1/2 cup flour, beat 2 minutes at high speed, scraping bowl occasionally. With spoon, stir in enough additional flour to make soft dough. Knead on lightly floured surface until smooth and elastic, about 4-6 minutes. Cover, let rest on floured surface 10 minutes. Divide dough in half. For body, knead chocolate morsels into 1 half, form into ball. Place on bottom end of large greased baking sheet; flatten to make 5-inch round. For head, remove 1/3 of remaining half, form into ball. Place on large baking sheet above body, flatten slightly, pinching to attach. For nose, pinch off 1/2 inch ball from remaining dough; place on center of head. Divide remaining dough into 4 equal portions, roll each to form 6-inch rope. For arms, arrange 2 ropes across body; attach by tucking one end of each under body. Shape remaining ropes into ears; arrange above head. Attach by tucking one end of each under head. Cover, let rise in warm draft-free place until doubled in size, about 30-45 minutes. Bake at 350 degrees for 45-50 minutes or until done, covering aluminum foil after 20 minutes to prevent excess browning. Remove from sheet; cool on wire rack. Decorate as desired.

Chocolate Cherry Bread

3/4 c Water
1 1/2 c White bread flour
1/2 c Wheat bread flour
1 tb Dry milk
2 tb Molasses
1 ts Salt
1/3 c Chocolate chips
1/3 c Cherries, dried
2 ts Triple Sec liquor
1/4 ts Orange peel
1 ts Yeast, fast rise or machine or 2 ts Yeast, active dry
Kids love it, but for adults, Chocolate Cherry turns a coffee break into a pleasant interlude. With a sweet topping, it becomes a new dessert bread.

Chocolate Chip and Nut Bread

1 1/2 c Whole Wheat Flour 1 1/2 c Bread Flour
2 tb Dry Milk
1 1/2 ts Sea Salt

1/3 c Toasted and Chopped Almonds 1/3 c Toasted and Ground Almonds 2/3 c Semisweet Choc. Chips
1 c Plus 3 tb. Water

3 tb Honey
2 tb Canola, Sunflower or Safflower Oil
1 ts Almond Extract
4 ts Active Dry Yeast
Add all ingred. at the same time according to your mfg. instructions. Bake on WHOLE WHEAT CYCLE.

Chocolate Chip Bread

1 pk Yeast
3 c Bread flour
2 tb Brown sugar
2 tb White sugar
1 ts Salt
1 ts Cinnamon
4 tb Soft butter
1 Egg
1 c Warm milk
1/4 c Water
1 c Chocolate chips

Put the first 10 ingredients into the pan, select white bread and push start. When the Auto Bakery "beeps" 5 minutes from the end of the second mixing, add the chocolate chips.

Chocolate Chip Grape Nut Bread

1 c Grape nuts
2 c Buttermilk (low fat 1.5%)
2 c Sugar
2 Eggs or 1/2c egg substitute
1/2 ts Salt
3 1/2 c Flour
1 ts Baking soda
2 ts Baking powder
1/2 c Chocolate chips
1 ts Nanilla

Soak Grape-Nuts in buttermilk for 10 minutes. Beat sugar and eggs or substitute together in a large bowl. Add milk/Grape-Nuts mixture and vanilla. Sift flour with salt, soda and powder and stir thoroughly into the Grape-Nuts mixture. Add chocolate chips and mix well. Pour into 2 non-stick sprayed 9 x 5 loaf pans and bake at 350 degrees F for about 45 minutes, or until a toothpick comes out clean. Makes 2 loaves, or about 20 servings.

Chocolate Chip Mandel Bread

3/4 c Sugar
1 c Oil
4 Eggs
3 1/2 c -4 cups flour 1 ts Baking powder 1 ts Nanilla

1 ts Almond flavoring
8 oz Shelled walnuts
12 oz Chocolate chips
In a large bowl, mix together the sugar, oil and eggs. Add the sifted flour, baking powder, vanilla and almond extracts, and mix well. Add the walnuts and the chocolate chips.

Mixture should be very thick and sticky. Shape into two loaves and place on either side of a cookie sheet. Bake at 325 degrees F for 30-35 minutes and then remove from oven. Cut into slices while still warm and return to the oven for another 5-10 minutes, or until slices are light brown.

Chocolate Coconut Bread

1 c Heavy cream
1 1/2 Eggs
3 tb Fruit juice concentrate
3 tb Honey
1 1/2 tb Unsweetened cocoa
1/3 ts Salt
1/3 c Coconut flakes
3 tb Nital gluten; optional
3/4 c Wheat flakes
3 c Whole wheat flour
1 1/2 ts Yeast
1/2 c Chocolate chips
1/3 c Chopped nuts
Use Raisin/Mix Cycle and add Chocolate Chips and Chopped nuts when indicated;
or 5 minutes prior to the end of the second kneading cycle

Chocolate Cream of Wheat Bread

1 1/2 pound loaf:
1 c Milk
3 tb Butter or margarine
1 1/2 Eggs
1 ts Salt (up to 1 1/2 ts)
1/3 c Sugar
1 1/2 tb Unsweetened cocoa
1 c Cream of wheat; uncooked
2 c Bread flour
1 1/2 ts Active dry yeast
1/3 c Chocolate chips; optional
2 pound loaf:
1 1/3 c Milk
4 tb Butter or margarine
2 Eggs
1 ts Salt (to 2 ts)
1/2 c Sugar
2 tb Unsweetened cocoa
1 1/3 c Cream of wheat; uncooked
2 2/3 c Bread flour
2 ts Active dry yeast
1/2 c Chocolate chips; optional
Add chocolate chips at the beep or appropriate time for your machine. Cycle:
white, sweet, raisin; no timer
Setting: light

Chocolate Lover's Breakfast Bread

3 c Flour 3 Eggs
2 c Sugar 1 c Oil

1 ts Nanilla
1 ts Each: ground cinnamon,
Baking Soda and baking powder
1/2 c Sour cream
2 c Shredded zucchini
1 c Semi-sweet chocolate bits
Combine flour, eggs, sugar, oil, vanilla, cinnamon, baking soda, baking powder
and sour cream in a mixing bowl. Beat at medium speed for 2 minutes or until
well blended. Stir in zucchini and chocolate bits. Pour batter into 2 well-greased
loaf pans and bake at 350 degrees for 1 hour and 15 minutes.

Chocolate Peanut Butter Banana Bread

Filling:
1/4 c Miniature choc. chips
1/4 c Flour
1/4 c Peanut butter
2 tb Sugar
Bread:
1 pk Pillsbury Banana Quick Bread Mix.
1 c Water
3 tb Oil
2 Eggs
1/4 c Mini choc. chips

Heat oven to 375 degrees. Grease and flour bottom only of 8x4 or 9x5 inch loaf pan In small bowl, combine all filling ingredients; mix well. Set aside. In large bowl, combine all bread ingredients except 1/4 cup choc. chips. Stir 50 to 75 strokes by hand until mix is moistened, stir in 1/4 cup choc. chips. Pour half of batter into greased and floured pan. Sprinkle filling evenly over batter, pour remaining batter over filling. Bake for 55 to 65 minutes for 8x4 inch pan; 45 to 55 minutes for 9x5 inch or until deep golden brown and toothpick inserted in center comes out clean. Cool 15 minutes; remove from pan. Cool completely. Wrap tightly and store in the refrigerator.

Chocolate Truffle Loaf With Raspberry Sauce

2 c Heavy cream
3 Egg yolks; slightly beaten
16 oz Baker's semisweet chocolate
1/2 c Lt. Karo syrup
1/2 c Butter
1/4 c Powdered sugar
1 ts Nanilla
Sauce:
10 oz Frozen raspberries; pureed and strained
1/3 c Lt. Karo corn syrup
Fresh raspberries for garnish
Line a loaf pan with plastic wrap. Mix a 1/2 C heavy cream with the egg yolks. In a 3 qt pan, melt chocolate, corn syrup and butter over medium heat. Add the egg mixture and cook 3 minutes, stirring constantly. Coll to room temperature. Beat the remaining heavy cream, sugar, and vanilla to soft peak stage. Fold into the chocolate mixture and pour into the lined pan. Refrigerate overnight. Stir the corn syrup into the raspberry puree. Remove chocolate loaf from pan. Serve sliced, topped with puree, a dollop of whipped cream, and a couple of fresh raspberries.

Chocolate Walnut Bread

1 Loaf 1 pound frozen bread dough
4 oz Semisweet chocolate, coarsely chopped
1/2 c Walnuts; chopped
3 tb Honey (or 2 tablespoons)
Preheat oven to 375 degrees. Thaw dough and let rise until twice its original size. Punch down and roll dough out to 6 x 12 inches. Sprinkle chocolate and nuts down the center of the dough, leaving about an inch on all sides. Pull long sides up towards the center and press to seal. Place dough, with seam side on the bottom, into stoneware loaf pan. Evenly spread honey over top. Bake for 50-60 minutes until crust is golden brown. Cool slightly in pan. Remove from pan and cool an additional 10-15 minutes before slicing. Yield: 1 loaf

Chocolate Zucchini Bread

3 Eggs
2 c White sugar
1 c Oil
2 Squares unsweetened chocolate, melted
1 ts Nanilla
2 c Grated zucchini
3 c Flour
1 ts Salt
1 ts Cinnamon
1 1/2 ts Baking powder
1 ts Baking soda
1 c Nuts, ground
Mix eggs, sugar and oil WELL!! Stir in melted chocolate and add vanilla and stir in zucchini. Add dry ingredients slowly and mix well. Pour into 2 9x5x3 inch greased loaf pans. Bake at 350 degrees for 50 minutes or until they test done. Cool and turn out on cake rack to finish cooling.

Chocolate Zucchini Nut Bread

1 c Salad Oil
3 ea Eggs
1 ts Salt
1/4 ts Baking Powder 1 ts Baking Soda

2 oz Baking Chocolate, Melted 2 c Grated, peeled Zucchini
1 c Chopped Nuts
2 c Sugar

3 c Flour
1 ts Cinnamon
1 ts Nanilla
1/2 c chocolate Chips
chocolate into egg mixture along with zucchini and vanilla. Sift flour with salt, cinnamon, baking powder and baking soda. With a large spoon, stir into zucchini mixture, along with nuts and chips. Mix thoroughly. Spoon into 2 well-greased 9" x 5" pans. Bake at 350 degrees F for 1 hr.

Orange Chocolate Chip Bread

1/2 c Skim milk
1/2 c Plain nonfat yogurt
1/3 c Sugar
1/4 c Orange juice
1 Egg; slightly beaten
1 tb Orange peel; freshly grated
3 c All-purpose biscuit baking m
1/2 c Hershey's mini chips semi-sweet

Heat oven to 350 degrees F. Grease 9 x 5 x 3-inch loaf pan or spray with vegetable cooking spray. In large bowl, stir together milk, yogurt, sugar, orange juice, egg and orange peel; add baking mix. With spoon, beat until well blended, about 1 min. Stir in small chocolate chips. Pour into prepared pan. Bake 45 to 50 mins or until a wooden pick inserted in center comes out clean. Cool 10 mins; remove from pan to wire rack. Cool completely before slicing. Garnish as desired. Wrap leftover bread in foil or plastic wrap. Store at room temperature or freeze for longer storage. Yield: 1 loaf (16 slices)

Orange Chocolate Tea Bread

1 Stick butter, softened
3/4 c Sugar
2 Eggs
1 tb Plus 1 tsp. grated orange zest
2 tb Orange liqueur such as Grand Marnier 3/4 c Half and half

2 c All-purpose flour
1 tb Baking powder
1/4 ts Salt
1/2 c Chopped walnuts
7 oz Semisweet chocolate, chopped 1 tb Water

Preheat oven to 350 degrees F. Grease or spray a 9x5x3 inch loaf pan. Cream together the butter and sugar until light and fluffy. Add the eggs and beat well. Beat in orange zest and 1 tablespoon of liqueur. Pour in half-and-half and beat to combine. (Do not be concerned with curdling.)

In another bowl, stir and toss together flour, baking powder, and salt. Add to butter mixture and gently beat just to combine. Stir in nuts and 4 ounces chopped chocolate. Spoon batter into prepared pan and smooth top. Bake 1 hour, until top is golden. Cool in pan on rack. Invert onto serving platter and cool completely.

When bread is cool, combine remaining chocolate with water and remaining tablespoon of orange liqueur in heavy saucepan. Place over low heat and melt, stirring constantly. Spread evenly over top and chill to set. Yield: 1 Loaf

Real Chocolate Bread

1 pk Yeast
3 c Flour, bread
1/2 c Sugar
1/4 c Unsweetened cocoa
1 Egg, unbeaten
1/4 c Soft butter or margarine
1/2 ts Nanilla
1 c Milk, warm
Add all the ingredients in the order given, select white bread, and push start.

Splendiferous Chocolate Dessert Bread

1 c Betty Crocker Super Moist Double Chocolate cake mix 1 c All purpose flour
1 c White bread flour
1/2 c Whole wheat bread flour

3 tb Gluten flour
2 tb Sugar
2 tb Oil
1 tb Swirl powder * 2 ts Yeast

1 lg Egg
1/4 c Liquid (half chocolate syrup and half water)
1 c Water
11 oz Mandarin oranges diced
1/3 c Chopped walnuts or almonds
2/3 c Chocolate chips **
1/2 c Coconuts (shredded)
1/3 c Maraschino cherries (diced
Or quartered)
* Swirl powder comes in a separate envelope with the cake mix. ** Use semi-sweet chips Adjust the amounts of fruit, nuts, and chips to suit.
Pat oranges and cherries dry between double layers of paper towels. Add fruits, nuts, and chips, at the beep or near the very end of the second kneading.
Nariations: Add more fruit. Use some juice from the oranges in place of water portion of liquid.
Serve plain as a snack or dessert, or, add your favorite topping for added enjoyment.

Super Chocolate Bread

1 c Tepid water, PLUS 1 Tablespoon 2 3/4 c Bread flour
2 tb Hot cocoa mix
1 1/2 tb Sugar

1 1/2 ts Salt
1 ts Cinnamon
2 tb Butter, or margarine
2 ts Active dry yeast
1 1/4 c Chocolate chips, added at the *beep
Put all ingredients in your bread maker in the order given by the manufacturer....
Use SWEET CYCLE.

Brownies

A. B. C. Brownies

1/2 c Butter
1 1/2 ts Baking powder
1 c Brown sugar -- packed
1/2 c Almonds -- coarsely chop
2 Eggs -- beaten
1 ts Nanilla extract
1/2 c Chocolate chips
1 1/2 c Flour

Melt butter in saucepan. Stir in brown sugar. Bring to a boil; turn off heat. Cool for 5-10 minutes. Rapidly stir in eggs, being careful not to cook them. A dd vanilla. In bowl, combine flour and baking powder. Stir into sugar-egg mix. Pour into a greased 8" square pan. Sprinkle with almonds and chocolate chips. Bake at 375 degrees F for 20 minutes.

Afternoon Tea Brownies

1 c Cake flower;
1/2 ts Salt;
1 ts Baking powder;
2 tb Cocoa;
1 oz Baking chocolate, melted;
1/4 c Negetable shortening;
3 Eggs;
1/2 c Granulated sugar replacement
1/2 c Skim milk;
1/2 c Pecans, toasted and ground;
Sift flower, salt, baking powder and cocoa together. Pour melted chocolate over shortening and stir until completely blended. Beat eggs until thick and lemon-colored; gradually add sugar replacement. Add chocolate mixture and small amount of flower mixture. Beat to thoroughly blend. Add remaining flour mixture alternately with the milk. Fold in the pecans. Spread in two 8-in. greased and paper-lined pans. Bake at 325 F for 17 to 20 minutes. Cut into 1 X 2 in. bars.

All Time Brownies

2/3 c Butter
4 tb Cocoa
1/2 c Fruit Sweet
2 Eggs
2/3 c Flour
1 ts Baking powder
1/4 ts Salt
1/2 c Nuts; chopped (opt)
Preheat the oven to 325 F. Spray a 9" square pan with a non-stick coating spray.
Blend the butter, cocoa, and Fruit Sweet. Add the eggs, one at a time, beating
well after each addition. Mix the flour, baking powder and salt; add to the
mixture. Fold in the nuts. Pour into the pan and bake 15 to 20 minutes, until the
brownies spring back when lightly touched in the center.

Almond Butter Brownies

1/2 c Almond butter 1 c Sugar
2 Eggs
1 ts Almond extract 1/2 c Flour

1/4 c Cocoa
1 ts Baking powder
1/4 ts Salt
1/2 c Grated coconut
Preheat the oven to 350. Combine the almond butter and sugar. Add the eggs and almond extract: mix well. In another bowl, combine the flour, cocoa, baking powder, and salt. Add the dry ingredients to the wet, and mix well. Stir in the coconut. Pour into a greased 9-inch square baking pan. Bake for 35 minutes.

Almond Macaroon Brownies

3 oz Cream cheese
6 tb Butter or margarine
3/4 c Sugar
3 Eggs
1/2 c Flour
1 tb Flour
1 2/3 c Flaked coconut
1 c Whole blanched almonds
6 oz Semisweet chocolate
1/2 ts Nanilla
1/2 ts Baking powder
1/4 ts Salt

Beat cream cheese and 2 tablespoons butter until softened. Beat in 1/4 cup sugar. Stir in 1 egg, 1 tablespoon flour and coconut. Reserve 16 whole almonds, chop the rest. Stir in 1/3 cup chopped almonds; set aside. Melt 5 oz chocolate and remaining butter (4 T) over low heat, until melted. Remove from heat. Stir in 1/2 cup sugar and vanilla. Beat in 2 eggs. Stir in 1/2 cup flour, baking powder and salt. Add remaining chopped almonds. Spread cheese batter on top. Garnish with whole almonds. Bake for 40 minutes until cake tester comes out clean, don't overbake. Melt remaining square of chocolate and drizzle over the brownies. Cool in pan. Cut into squares. Recipe can be doubled.

Almost Fat Free Brownies

1/2 c Unsweetened Cocoa Powder 4 oz Jar Prune Baby Food
3 Egg Whites
1 c Sugar

1 ts Salt
1 ts Nanilla
1/2 c Flour
1/4 c Nuts -- (optional)
Preheat oven to 350 degrees. Spray an 8-inch square baking pan with cooking spray. Combine all ingredients. Add nuts if desired. Bake about 30 minutes or until springy to touch. Cool on rack.
Cut into 16 pieces.

Ark Brownies

1 lb Butter
3/4 lb Semi-sweet chocolate,(12 sq)
3 c Flour (minus 6 Tbsp.)
2 1/4 t Nanilla
7 Eggs
4 c Sugar
4 c Walnuts, chopped
Preheat oven to 350. Over low heat, melt butter and chocolate. Remove from heat. Stir in flour and vanilla. With mixer, whip eggs and sugar until mixture resembles a yellow ribbon. Blend in chocolate mixture on slow speed. Stir in walnuts. Spread batter into a greased 9X13" and a greased 8" square pan. Bake 35 minutes for large pan: 30 minutes for small pan. Makes 3 1/2 dozen.

Award Winner Brownies

2 Eggs
3/4 c Sugar
1 ts Nanilla
1/2 c Butter or margarine; melted
3/4 c Chocolate; ground
2/3 c Unsifted flour
1/4 ts Baking powder
1/4 ts Salt
1/2 c Walnuts; chopped

Heat oven to 350 degrees F. Using a spoon, stir eggs with sugar and vanilla; add butter. Sift Ground Chocolate with flour, baking powder and salt. Stir into egg mixture; add nuts. Spread into greased 8 or 9" square pan. Bake at 350 degrees F for 20-30 minutes. For extra chewy brownies, use 8" pan and less baking time. For cake like brownies use 9" pan and longer baking. Cut into squares.

Banana Berry Brownie Pizza

1/3 c Cold water
1 15 oz pkg. brownie mix
1/4 c Oil
1 Egg
8 oz Phila. Brand Cream Cheese, softened
1/4 c Sugar
1 Egg
1 ts Nanilla
Strawberry slices
Banana slices
2 1 oz squares Baker's semi-sweet chocolate, melted
Preheat oven to 350 degrees. Bring water to a boil. Mix together brownie mix, water, oil and egg in large bowl til well blended. Pour into greased, floured 12 inch pizza pan. Bake 25 minutes. Beat cream cheese sugar, egg and vanilla in small mixing bowl at medium speed til well blended. Pour over crust. Bake 15 minutes. Cool. Top with fruit. Drizzle with chocolate. Garnish with mint leaves if desired.

Banana Cream Brownie Squares

3/4 c Dry roasted peanuts; chopped 15 oz Brownie mix
2 md Banana; sliced
1 1/4 c Milk

5 1/8 oz Instant vanilla pudding & pie filling 8 oz Cool whip(r); thawed
9 Strawberries; optional
1 oz Unsweetened baking chocolate, optional 1 md Banana; optional

Prepare brownie mix according to package directions & stir in 1/2 cup chopped peanuts. Pour into a greased 9 inch square pan. Bake at 350F for 24-27 minutes. Cool completely.
Layer 2 of the sliced bananas over the brownie. Whisk pudding mix & milk together until pudding just begins to thicken. Fold in 2 1/2 cups Cool Whip. Quickly spread pudding mixture over the sliced bananas. Refrigerate 30 minutes.

Sprinkle remaining 1/4 cup peanuts over pudding mixture.
To serve: Pipe remaining Cool Whip over the squares. Grate chocolate over the dessert. Top each square with banana & strawberry slices.

Banana-brownies, Lo Cal

1 c Flour, all purpose
1/4 c Nonfat dry milk powder
1/4 ts Salt
1 c Sugar
1/4 c Buttermilk
1/3 c Coca, unsweetened
1/4 ts Baking soda
1 ea Large very ripe banana
2 ea Large egg whites
1 ts Nanilla

Preheat oven 350F. Coat 9 in. square baking pan with vegetable cooking spray. Combine flour, cocoa, milk powder, baking soda and salt in bowl. Puree banana, sugar, egg whites, buttermilk and vanilla in food processor until smooth. Add dry ingredients and pulse just until blended. Pour into prepared pan. Bake 25 minutes or until toothpick comes out clean. Cut into 2 in. squares.

Beacon Hill Brownies

8 oz Unsweetened chocolate 1 c Butter
5 Eggs
3 c Sugar

1 tb Nanilla
1 1/2 c Flour
2 c Walnuts; coarsely chopped
Melt chocolate with butter in saucepan over very low heat; stirring constantly until smooth. Cool slightly. Beat eggs, sugar, and vanilla in a large mixing bowl at high speed 10 min. Blend in chocolate at low speed. Add flour, beating just to blend. Stir in walnuts. Spread in greased 13x9" pan. Bake at 375 degree For 35-40 minutes. (do not overbake). Cool in pan. Cut into bars or squares. Makes 24-32

Beanie Brownies

1 c Brown tepary beans; cooked 1/2 c Carob powder;
3/4 c Mild honey;
1/4 c Margarine; melted

1/2 c Flour, all-purpose; 1/2 c Walnuts, chopped; 1/2 c Raisins (optional) 2 Eggs; well beaten

1 1/2 ts Nanilla essence;
1/2 ts Salt;
Butter an 8 inch square pan. Line with waxed paper and butter the paper. Whirl the tepary beans in a food processor until smooth. In a large bowl, mix the processed beans with rest of the ingredients. Spread in prepared baking dish. Bake at 325 degrees F for 30 to 35 minutes. Cool, before removing from the pan. Peel off waxed paper and cut into squares. Makes 16 2 inch squares.

Best Chocolate Brownies

1 c Butter or margarine
4 oz Unsweetened chocolate
2 c Sugar
4 Eggs
1 c All purpose flour
2 ts Nanilla
1 ts Baking powder
1 c Chopped walnuts
1 c Semi-sweet chocolate

In a 2 quart saucepan melt butter or margarine and unsweetened chocolate over low heat. Transfer chocolate mixture to a large mixer bowl.

Add sugar, mix well, add eggs, one at a time, beating just till blended. In a mixing bowl stir together flour and baking powder. Add to chocolate mixture along with the vanilla, mix well. Pour batter into a greased and floured 13x9x2 inch baking pan. Sprinkle with the chopped walnuts and chocolate pieces. Bake in oven at 325 degrees F about 45 minutes or till done. Let cool on a wire rack. Cut into bars.

Best Chocolate Syrup Brownies

1/2 c Butter 1 c Sugar
3 Eggs
ds Salt

1 c All purpose flour
3/4 c Chocolate syrup -- canned
2 tb Nanilla extract
3/4 c Chopped pecans
Pecans for garnish
Cream together butter, sugar and eggs until creamy and well blended. Add salt.
Stir in flour, mixing to blend. Add chocolate syrup, vanilla and chopped pecans.
Turn mixture into well greased and lightly floured 9" square pan. Smooth top.
Bake at 350 degrees for about 35 minutes until stick inserted near center comes
out clean. Cool in pan on wire rack but loosen cake at edges, cut into squares.
Garnish with pecan halves, dust with powdered sugar.

Bisquick Fudge Brownies

2 c Chocolate chips
1/4 c Margarine
2 c Biscuit baking mix
1 cn Sweetened condensed milk
1 Eggs; beaten
1 ts Nanilla

Preheat oven to 350 degrees F. In large saucepan, over low heat, melt 1 cup chips with margarine; remove from heat. Add biscuit mix, condensed milk, egg and vanilla. Stir in remaining chips. Turn into well-greased 13x9" pan. Bake 20 to 25 minutes or until brownies begin to pull away from sides of pan. Cool. Garnish as desired. Cut into bars.

Black & White Brownies

1 c Cake flour
1 ts Baking powder
1/4 ts Salt
1/2 c Shortening, softened
1/2 c Granulated sugar replacement
2 Eggs
1 ts Nanilla extract
1 tb Water
1/4 c Unsweetened coconut, grated
1 ts Coconut milk
1 oz Baking chocolate, melted

Sift together the flour, baking powder and salt. Cream shortening and sugar replacement until light and fluffy.

Add eggs, one at a time, beating well after each addition. Beat in vanilla extract and water.

Divide batter into two equal parts. To one part add unsweetened coconut and coconut milk. Stir to completely blend. To the remaining half, beat in the melted chocolate.

Spread coconut mixture on bottom of well-greased 8-in square pan. Spread chocolate layer on top of coconut layer. Bake at 350 degrees F for 25 to 30 min. Cut into 1 x 2 inch bars.

Black Forest Brownies A La Mode

21 1/2 oz Brownie mix
1 c Cherry pie filling
1/4 c Oil
2 Egg whites -- whipped
1 c Semisweet chocolate chips
2 c Low-fat vanilla ice cream

Preheat oven to 350. prepare a 13 x 9" pan with cooking spray and flour; set aside. In a mixing bowl, combine brownie mix, cherry pie filling, oil, and egg whites. Pour into prepared pan. Bake for 30 minutes. Remove from oven, sprinkle with chocolate chips, spread when melted.

Blockbuster Brownies

8 Squares unsweetened chocolate 1 1/2 c Butter or margarine
6 Eggs
3 c Granulated sugar

1 1/2 c Flour
1 tb Nanilla
1 c Chopped walnuts
Melt chocolate and butter or margarine over hot water or in microwave on medium 4 minutes. Cool. Beat eggs until lemon colored. Gradually add sugar, beating until thick about 3 minutes. Stir in chocolate mixture, fold in flour, vanilla and nuts. Pour into two greased 2 l square pans. Bake at 350 for 35 to 40 minutes. Toppings: Sprinkle with chopped nuts and semi sweet chocolate chips before baking. Sprinkle cool Brownies with icing sugar
Glaze: Melt 1 square of unsweetened chocolate with 1 tb of butter and 1/4 cup of milk, blend until smooth. Add 1 1/4 cup of icing sugar, blend well. Spread over pan cooled brownies. Rocky Road: Sprinkle 2 cups miniature marshmallows over 1 pan of brownies. Broil under preheated broiler until golden brown. Drizzle with 1 square melted semi sweet chocolate.

Blond Brownies

8 oz (1)pkg white cake mix; NO-SUGAR
2 Eggs;
2 tb Granulated brown sugar; REPLACEMENT
2 tb Water
1/4 c Mints chocolate chips;
1/4 c Peanut butter chips;
Combine cake mix, eggs, brown sugar REPLACEMENT and water in mixing bowl.
Beat in medium speed until well blended and thickened. Fold in chips. Pour batter
into two, greased and papered 8-in pans. Bake at 375 degrees for 12 to 15
minutes or until brownies test done. Cut into 2-in squares.

Blondies

6 tb Butter
3/4 c Light brown sugar
1 Egg
1 tb Milk
1 ts Nanilla
1 c Flour
1/2 ts Soda
1/8 ts Salt
10 oz Chocolate chunks or chips
1/2 c Nuts; chopped (opt)
Mix flour, soda and salt, set aside. Cream butter, sugar, brown sugar and vanilla.
Add flour mix and beat until creamy. Add chocolate chips and nuts if desired.
Bake in 9x9" pan at 350~ for 20-25 minutes.

Bombshell Brownies

3 Cloves garlic; finely chopped 1/2 c Butter
1 c Unsweetened cocoa
4 Eggs; lightly beaten

1 c Sugar (some of it brown, if you prefer) 1 c Flour; sifted
3/4 c Walnuts; chopped
1/3 c Almonds; blanched

Preheat oven to 325F. Put the garlic and butter into a large bowl over a saucepan of water on a gentle heat. When the butter has melted, stir in the cocoa and mix well. Add the eggs, sugar, flour and walnuts, stirring well after each addition. Pour the mixture into a greased and floured 8X10 inch cake pan and decorate with the blanched almonds. Bake for approx. 35 minutes. The top should be springy, but the inside slightly moist. Turn out onto a wire rack and cut into squares or bars.